# Exploring Indigenous Spirituality:
*The Kutchi Kohli Christians of Pakistan*

# Exploring Indigenous Spirituality:
## *The Kutchi Kohli Christians of Pakistan*

A Journey of Adaptation and Creativity

## Anita Maryam Mansingh

*Foreword by Noelia Molina*

WIPF & STOCK · Eugene, Oregon

EXPLORING INDIGENOUS SPIRITUALITY: THE KUTCHI KOHLI
CHRISTIANS OF PAKISTAN
A Journey of Adaptation and Creativity

Copyright © 2021 Anita Maryam Mansingh. All rights reserved. Except for brief quotations in critical publications or reviews, no part of this book may be reproduced in any manner without prior written permission from the publisher. Write: Permissions, Wipf and Stock Publishers, 199 W. 8th Ave., Suite 3, Eugene, OR 97401.

Wipf & Stock
An Imprint of Wipf and Stock Publishers
199 W. 8th Ave., Suite 3
Eugene, OR 97401

www.wipfandstock.com

PAPERBACK ISBN: 978-1-6667-0736-6
HARDCOVER ISBN: 978-1-6667-0737-3
EBOOK ISBN: 978-1-6667-0738-0

07/29/21

Cover photo by Emmanuel Guddu.

To my parents, Mansingh Rawa and Rani Moti, and to all those Kutchi Kohlis who day by day search for their roots, build their present, and shape their future.

نيڪري سون هون أوني ڳوچ مان
زين کهوال پڙي سي الاني سال مور ني شيلي مان

ڪائين خبر نٿي آ ڳوچ چان لني زائي مونين
بس هيمچ تو جام سي انين اُنسين سي ماري أوڏ

ايڪ ڪچهي ڪوري سون ٻنون هون پوتاني قوم ني آواز
چون قوم نين هون إي اوركائڻ زين ٿي ٿاني أنسون إي نون مان

نا ٻيڪ مونين ڪونين ني،نا ڳٺتي آڏون پڙوا وارا ني
هون تو سون پوتي أو، زين نين آڳر طوفان ٻڻ ڪانين ني

هون چيم پولون ماري قوم نين زين ٿي ديدون زلم مونين
رنيش هون هميش آڳراؤپي روڪش هندائين خطره نين

زيم ٿاني مون ٿي أونيا نون وڪائڻ
ايمز سي أونيان ٿي ماري اوركائڻ

I have started my search for what is hidden in the dust of centuries
I have no idea where this search is going to take me
I am a dreamer and in my dream for my people I soar high
I am a Kutchi Kohli and I become a voice for them
I may give them the recognition which raises their dignity
I am so on fire for their welfare that I'm blind to obstacles
I am that kind of soul in front of whom, the storms are not a problem
How can I forget my people who have given me life
I will always stand like a shield to protect them from danger
As they are being known through me,
I am known through them.

**By Anita Maryam**

# Contents

*List of Figures* | ix
*Foreword by Noelia Molina* | xi
*Preface* | xv
*Acknowledgments* | xix
*Introduction* | xxiii
    Aim and Objectives | xxiv
    Definitions | xxv
    Outline of the Chapters | xxix

1. **Encountering and Understanding the Kutchi Kohli Christians** | 1
    The Kutchi Kohli Christian | 1
    Complementary Conceptual Tools of Analysis | 9
    Summary | 16

2. **A Narrative Approach to the Spiritual Life of the Kutchi Kohli Christians** | 17
    Methodology Framework | 17
    Spirituality Framework | 21

3. **Kutchi Kohli Voices and the Shaping of Their Identity** | 27
    Kutchi Kohli Christian Identity and *Kutchikohliness* | 28
    Building a Relationship with God:
        The Shaping of Interiority | 35

      Community and Family: A Ground
         for Spiritual Growth | 38
      Interacting with People of Other Religions | 41
      Challenges and Obstacles for
         Spiritual Growth and Life | 44

4. **Paths towards the Future** | 50
      Expected and Unexpected Results | 50
      Emerging Themes and Existing Literature | 53
      Strengths and Limitations | 54
      Further Research | 55
      Recommendations | 56
      Conclusion | 58

*Appendix 1: Questionnaire in English* | 61
*Appendix 2: Data Analysis Procedure and Thematic Results* | 63
*Appendix 3: Photos of Kutchi Kohlis* | 67
*Glossary* | 71
*Bibliography* | 73

# List of Figures

Figure 1: Map of Sindh Province, Pakistan | 3

Figure 2: Kutchi Kohli Christians in the Pakistani Islamic Context | 10

Figure 3: Process of Data Analysis with NVivo | 21

Figure 4: Kutchi Kohli Christian Dynamic Process of Self-Awareness | 23

Figure 5: Authenticity and Resilience as a Grill of Analysis | 25

Figure 6: Identity Relation of Kutchi Kohli Christian with Their *Kutchikholiness* | 26

Figure 7: Identity Processes among Kutchi Kohli Christians | 54

Figure 8: Kutchi Kohli Woman Preparing Food | 67

Figure 9: Kutchi Kohli Christian Wedding | 68

Figure 10: Kutchi Kohli Christian Wedding | 68

Figure 11: Kutchi Kohli Christian Couple Performing *Fera* | 69

# Foreword

IN THIS BOOK, ANITA has managed to depict a spiritual map that is quite crucial for the Kutchi Kohli and is also humanly universal. Every time a cultural practice ceases to exist or a minority language isn't spoken anymore, a part of us all is lost. Nothing has been written on the Kutchi Kohli spirituality. Writing this book is walking on uncharted territory, as all Kutchi Kohli practices are transmitted orally.

She did a conscious study on other indigenous spiritualities in Israel, Latin America, and Thailand. This study pioneers complex, profound concepts on how to research indigenous spirituality: interspirituality, multiple or double religious belonging, and hybridization. The process of enculturation and the process by which cultures become fluid are intricate. This book is a profound study on how to create a conceptual framework that helps to analyze Kutchi Kohli spirituality.

Anita underwent a deep, organic journey to explore through her own native language the process of constructing meaning and identity in which she was also embedded. She has done this beautifully and exquisitely for her people. The quality of writing is highly academic and artistic at the same time. Anita is also a poet, and one can sense this in how she writes prose. She became her people's "voice" by conducting excellent interviews and by extracting the essence and the intricate social, historical, economical, emotional and spiritual substratum of her people. In a very original way, Anita encapsulated this intricacy by coining a neologism, *Kutchikohliness*.

By naming these unique experiences, the meaning of them becomes alive and they are given an existence of their own.

Every chapter in this book engages the reader on multiple levels. The narrative challenges us to dwell inside ourselves and encounter the cultural and spiritual life of Kutchi Kohli Christians. It forces us to overcome our colonial, religious, and social prejudices. It also makes us reflect on the crucial, historical, dual dynamics of the oppressor and the oppressed. I find Anita's book very timely. We are living through a world pandemic in which the concepts of healing, power, and oppression are at the front lines of discussion. The chair of the UN urged "Member States and the international community to include the specific needs and priorities of indigenous peoples in addressing the global outbreak of COVID-19."[1] As we know, indigenous peoples have an intimate relationship with the Earth and have been sealing their territories to facilitate isolation. They are vulnerable, and we cannot afford to lose the immense cultural heritage that may disappear with indigenous minority groups.

As Anita points out in her book, the Kutchi Kholi share common issues with other indigenous groups around the world. Economically, they are very poor. They are caught up in a feudal system as landless farmers, earning extremely low salaries which made it impossible to get out of the vicious cycle of debt to the landowners. They are manipulated and taken advantage of because of their lack of education. Therefore, the importance of this book and the fact that it is written by a Kutchi Kohli is in the hope that unfolds by naming and bringing to light the experiences and challenges of this minority group. In this sense, Linda Tuhiwai Smith points out, in her book *Decolonizing Methodologies*, that

> thirteen years ago when the book was published the worlds of indigenous peoples and research intersected only to the extent that indigenous communities were most often the objects or subjects of study by non-indigenous researchers. They were not considered agents themselves,

---

1. "COVID-19 and Indigenous Peoples."

as capable of or interested in research, or as having expert knowledge about themselves and their conditions.[2]

How can the Kutchi Kohli build a project of life integration? Certainly the main issue that comes to the forefront is education. Anita is a Presentation Sister. The transformative spirituality of their Irish founder, Nano Nagle, was about empowerment to the people who were pushed to the margins by poverty or dispossession. The power of education will free the individual and, by extension, the social group. Having conversations with Anita, I realized she has dreams for her people. She would love to build a heritage center for the Kutchi Kohli in her region. This project will achieve the permanence of their history and culture.

Most importantly, I believe, the concrete visualization of her people to everyone creates and builds a renew self-esteem for the entire community to feel proud of their roots, their very existence. This book is the first building block in constructing the new chapter in the history of the Kutchi Kohli. It also achieves the most needed reconciliation towards the harmonious relationships among Kutchi Kohlis, both Christian and Hindu. Spiritual and cultural healing is the drive for this research. I truly hope that readers can sense the dual spiritual transformation emerging in this book: that of the author and, by extension, that of her people, the Kutchi Kohli of Pakistan.

**Noelia Molina**
SpIRE (Spirituality Institute for Research and Education)
Dublin 2020

---

2. Smith, *Decolonizing Methodologies*, x.

# Preface

MY STUDY OF KUTCHI Kohli Christian spirituality has been not only an academic endeavor; it has also been an existential journey. In a certain way, the research questions about the characteristics, dynamics, and perspectives of Kutchi Kohli Christian spirituality were also questions about my own self, my own experience of God, my own personal and social journey.

I am a Kutchi Kohli, I am a Christian, I am a Pakistani, I am a woman, I am a religious sister (a member of a Catholic religious congregation, the Presentation Sisters). I imagine that I could make this list longer, but I think these five dimensions of my being express the complexity not only of who I am but also of who we are, the Kutchi Kohli Christians. We, I, have to articulate these multiple identities, these multiple belongings, constantly and creatively; our present and future are related to how we choose to integrate—or not to integrate—this diversity. Furthermore, each one of these dimensions refers in itself to complex realities that influence the way in which Kutchi Kohlis perceive themselves. In this perspective, this research has been for me a process of growth in awareness of the images that I have of myself and the images that we, the Kutchi Kohlis, have of ourselves.

In the same vein, since childhood I have heard multiple voices trying to tell us who we are: tribal people, semi-Christians, low caste, high caste, poor people, strong people, welcoming people, people who refuse education and changes . . . many labels, but not only labels. I have been excluded from school activities just precisely for who I am—and I am unhappily sure many of my brother and sister Kutchi Kohlis have gone through similar or more painful experiences. These labels and experiences leave deep wounds in one's memory, soul, and even body, but I think one of the most painful wounds is that of silence. This is not the silence of meditation, or contemplation, or wisdom, but the silence created by not having the opportunity to express, to say who we are and what we feel. This forced silence is a reality that surrounds us— Kutchi Kohlis, women, Christians in Pakistan. It is a silence that overshadows the richness of Pakistan and its people. I think that the most interesting and at the same time the most transformative experience for me during this research has been listening to the voice of other Kutchi Kohlis. Listening to the ways in which they make sense of the world in which they live, their experiences of the divine, and the ways in which they articulate being Christian and being Kutchi Kohli has not only allowed me to apprehend the complexity and richness of the spiritual life of the Kutchi Kohli Christians but has also transformed my understanding of spirituality itself. Thus, I am now more attentive, more aware of the multiple ways in which my cultural and ethnic identities shape my spiritual life on a deeper level, not only at the level of devotional or ritual practices.

This awareness of my roots has led me to consider the urgency of healing as a condition of possibility for development and for human and spiritual growth. I do not refer only to physical healing, in which the Christian churches and the Pakistani government continue to make efforts for providing access to everybody in Pakistan through education, health, and other social services. I refer to the healing of memories—the healing of the memory held in the body, in the soul, and in the mind.

Finally, I would like to point out that this research has not only opened multiple perspectives for personal growth, academic research, and empowerment of Kutchi Kohli Christians, it has also deepened an existential and academic question—who are we, the Kutchi Kohlis of Pakistan? This question is not only a historical question, it is also an identity question in the sense of Paul

*Preface*

Ricoeur's *Oneself as Another*—a question for what remains and what is constantly changing in our personal and collective identity. I think that this is a central question for us Kutchi Kohlis in Pakistan. Hopefully the attempt answer this question may lead us to be open to change and to avoid any useless efforts to remain isolated. Hopefully, it will also help us to continue existing as a people, as a community, in a world that is changing and in a context in which diversity is seen as a problem.

**Anita Maryam Mansingh**

# Acknowledgments

WITH GOD'S HELP I have finished this book, but throughout this journey, many people have played a most helpful role, and I wish to thank them all.

I am very thankful to my supervisor, Dr. Noelia Molina, whose constructive support gave me the courage to continue my journey. I appreciate her tireless generosity and dedication of her time to me. I have been privileged with her gentle presence and gracious help. To complete this book is a great achievement which would not have been possible without her being with me on my journey.

Thank you Dr. Michael O'Sullivan, SJ, for your authentic presence and support, which have taught me the true meaning of authenticity, subjectivity, and objectivity during this academic year. It does not only help me in the academic field but also in my personal path through life. I am going to carry it with me wherever I go so that I can hopefully leave the same mark of authenticity on the heart and soul of others as you have left on me.

Thank you Dr. Bernadette Flanagan, PBVM, for your gentle and serene presence, during the classes and throughout the year, which taught me the lesson that no matter how difficult a task or work may be, it can be done with calmness and consistency. In other words, there is always a way to do things if we are ready; what matters is having the courage to make a beginning, and the rest will fall into shape by itself. The methodology you taught us has been a vital component of this research.

*Acknowledgments*

Sincere thanks to all the lecturers who helped me not only in my academic growth but also in my personal and spiritual growth and taught me the meaning of applied spirituality. Thanks to Dr. Noelia Molina and David Halpin for your creativity in presenting each class of the Spiritual Accompaniment module and providing multiple articles which opened new perspectives for me. Besides this, the practical part of it built my confidence, which is going to remain with me for the rest of my life. Regarding the module "Contemporary Writers," which taught me how to look for spirituality in any book I read, thanks to David Halpin. Thanks to Anne Marie Dixon for her creativity during the sessions and her support and encouragement during the year. A sincere word of thanks to Brian Doony's interesting lectures, which helped me to connect spirituality with literature and music. Thanks to Amanda Dillon for her lectures on "Spirituality, Art and Imagination," which were both profound and inspiring. I wish to thank Fr. Jack Finnegan, SDB, for his soul- and mind-changing module that helped me to understand myself in a clearer way. Thanks to all the other lecturers who shared their knowledge with us, and my gratitude to the librarians of Milltown, who were most kind and helpful in finding the books and articles during my master's.

Sincere thanks to Fr. Tomás King, SSC, and Fr. Brendan Mulhall, MHM, from Sindh, Pakistan, for sharing their research with me. Heartfelt gratitude and thanks to Michael Liston, CSSp, and Fr. Juan Carlos, SJ, for being ever obliging friends whenever I needed their time and expertise. I really appreciate their availability and encouragement. Along with it, I would like to thank the Spiritans working in Sindh, Pakistan, who without any delay provided me with all the material relevant to my research that was within their reach.

Thanks to my spiritual director, Fr. Myles O'Reilly, SJ, who gave me his time and encouraged me with his gentle presence and positivity to move forward on my life's journey.

Thanks to my community—Srs. Lillie O'Reilly, Elizabeth Maxwell, Dympna O'Connell, Anne Kearney, and Breda

*Acknowledgments*

O'Shea—who with their presence and support have helped me feel at home throughout this year of study and growth.

Thanks to Fr. Edson Paguntalan, MHM, who was very kind in rendering his help any time I asked for it and even arranged a suitable place for the research interviews. Thanks to all the participants, who happily and willingly trusted me with their personal sharing without which this book would not have been enriching.

I am deeply indebted to my parents and family for their constant love and for being with me always. In a special way, I would like to pay gratitude to my late uncle Fr. Mohan Victor, OFM; he is with us no more, but I have always felt his presence with me and his constant guidance and support, which I experienced through my dreams and which have been the fuel that kept me going without giving up.

A sincere thanks to my Provincial, Sr. Emer Manning, and the leadership team—Srs. Teresa Baily, Margaret Patras, Rehana Mehnga, and Abida Sadiq—for giving me this opportunity to do my masters in applied spirituality.

Last but not least, my heartfelt gratitude to my classmate for their friendship and encouragement. Moreover, thanks to my triad, where we shared our personal and deep experiences. Thanks for trusting me and creating an atmosphere of openness.

# Introduction

PAKISTAN IS A LAND of multiple religions and cultures in which the interior life of peoples is devotionally expressed in many and colorful ways, but also through poetry, mystical, and philosophical texts. From this richness, Muslim spirituality, especially Sufism, has been studied from different perspectives. However, Pakistani Christianity has received lesser attention; its diversity, dynamics, and especially its spirituality have not been fully studied yet.[1] This research purposes to contribute to lessen this lacuna through the study of a particular community of Pakistani Christians—the Kutchi Kohli Christians.

    I have two main reasons for choosing to explore the spirituality of Kutchi Kohli Christians. Firstly, the Kutchi Kohli Christian community is a small, young, vibrant, and growing community among the Pakistani Christians. Its history and characteristics

---

    1. Fr. John Rooney wrote a comprehensive history of Christianity in Pakistan from the tenth century up to the twentieth century in multiple volumes. Volume 6 of this collection is dedicated to the history of the Catholic Church in Sindh and Baluchistan. This is an important contribution, and it has established the basis for further research. However, Rooney's work is not specifically focus on the Kutchi Kohli Christians, neither is it a study of their characteristics. Cf. Rooney, *Shadows in the Dark*; Rooney, *Symphony on Sands*. Similar monographs have been written specially concerning Christianity in the Pakistani province of Punjab; for instance: Stock and Stock, *People Movements in the Punjab*; Young, *Days of Small Things?* It is also important to mention that some books have been written on the history of particular congregations who have been present in Sindh and who have worked among the Kutchi Kohlis and Parkari Kohlis; an example of this is McKenna and Lordan, *Pakistan Presentation Story*.

xxiii

*Introduction*

have not been studied sufficiently, and the specific area of their spirituality has not been the object of serious study to date. Furthermore, the Kutchi Kohli Christians, as well as the Parkari Kohli Christians, find themselves at a particular social and religious crossroads. Thus, their Hindu origin is constantly in interaction with the Islamic context of Pakistan as well as in dialogue with the larger ethnic group among the Pakistani Christians, the Punjabi Christians. In this framework, on the one hand their position is one of fragility by reason of their number, their newness as Christians, and their socioeconomic position, and on the other hand, their creativity for making sense of their Christian identity in dialogue with their past and with the different actors of their present milieu makes of them active actors of their destiny. Secondly, there is a personal dimension in this choice; I am a Kutchi Kohli and the first who has become a professed religious Sister. Thus, to explore the spirituality of Kutchi Kohli Christians is also to explore my own roots, to make sense, in a certain way, of my experience of God and of my personal spiritual journey. Finally, I think it is also important to mention that the desire to contribute to the healing and growth of my own people has played an important role in choosing this topic. To understand the ways in which they relate to the divine can enlighten the ways in which pastoral agents can walk with them on their spiritual journeys.

## Aim and Objectives

The aim of this research is to conduct a case study of contemporary Kutchi Kohli Christian spirituality through an in-depth, detailed, qualitative study of a small group of individuals with a view to providing resources for the community's empowerment. It is important to indicate that this research will be limited to Catholic Kutchi Kohlis.[2]

---

2. Although the research is limited to Catholic Christians, I will use the term "Kutchi Kohli Christians" throughout the research because I think that (i) many characteristics and experiences are shared by Christians of different denominations, and (ii) that in order to understand their spiritual experience it is central

*Introduction*

As subsidiary objectives, this research proposes:

- To describe the main characteristics of the Kutchi Kohli ethnic group as an indigenous people.
- To identify the principal characteristics of the spirituality of the Kutchi Kohli Christians.
- To identify what is specific to the spiritual life of Kutchi Kohli Christians in relation to the Hindu majority of Kutchi Kohlis.
- To explore the influence of the Islamic context upon the spirituality of Kutchi Kohli Christians.
- To describe the elements (ways of expressing, praying, relating to the divine) that are empowering.
- To apply a conceptual framework of (i) indigenous spirituality, (ii) inter-spirituality—double religious belonging, and (iii) hybridization to analyze the spirituality of the Kutchi Kohli Christians.
- To analyze, in relation to the Islamic context of Pakistan, if the concept of "hybridization" is a more appropriate category for deepening Kutchi Kohli Christian spirituality or if we are facing a syncretic experience.

## Definitions

### Definition of "Indigenous" and Use of the Term

For many years various terms have been used to refer to groups of people who nowadays are considered "indigenous people." However, none of them has been considered adequate enough in academia. Thus, terms such as "primitive,"[3] "pre-literate" or "non-literate,"[4] or "tribal"[5] have been rejected by scholars as

---

to use the terms of self-reference, which in this case is "Christians."

3. Harvey, *Indigenous Religions*, 7.
4. Harvey, *Indigenous Religions*, 8.
5. Harvey, *Indigenous Religions*, 10.

*Introduction*

inappropriate to describe the reality of indigenous people. Ann Marie Bahr points out that "the United Nations (UN) uses the term *indigenous* to describe these people, but some individual governments use other designations such as *aboriginal* or *tribal*."[6] Moreover, the difficulties do not stop here concerning the appropriate terminology for referring to these groups of people; there is also the challenge of the content of these terms. What does indigenous mean? Can a single term describe the rich, diverse, and complex reality of these groups of people? This is not a minor challenge for this research. There are valid questions: On which ground is it possible to call the Kutchi Kohli indigenous people? Is it possible to speak of them as indigenous people when the Kutchi Kohlis are both Christians and Hindus? Is it appropriate to stop using the term "tribal" for referring to the Kutchi Kohlis?

I would like to consider some important elements that form part of the definition of "indigenous" in order to assess its suitability for use when referring to the Kutchi Kohlis of Pakistan. First, the relation to a particular land is part of the definition of "indigenous," as the UN's definition states: "Indigenous people are persons who live on their lands before settlers came from elsewhere."[7] This particular relation to the land is central to the definition of "indigenous" even in the cases of people belonging to these groups who have been forced to move to another land as a consequence of colonization, discrimination, or socioeconomic need. Considering this, it is possible to state that the Kutchi Kohli people have been related to this geographical area (land) in interaction with other ethnic groups for a long time prior to the creation of Pakistan and India and even before the arrival of Christianity and Islam in this region. Second, "indigenous" makes reference to a particular relation to the divine/supernatural, especially in relation to nature and its forces/expression. However, the advance of the so-called "world religions" has resulted in a situation where many indigenous people have accepted or been forcefully converted to Christianity,

---

6. Bahr, *Indigenous Religions*, 3.
7. Bahr, *Indigenous Religions*, 3.

*Introduction*

Hinduism, or Islam.[8] This point is particularly important for the Kutchi Kohli case study because I will be dealing with a group of people of whom the majority are Hindu—although some of them have become Christian—right throughout their known history. They have not lost their particular way of relating to their environment and to others. Consequently, it is important to explore the particularity and potential of the Kutchi Kohli from the perspective of indigenous spirituality.

Finally, the impossibility of reducing reality to one concept makes unthinkable an agreement on what is the most appropriate term. Nevertheless, Harvey points out an important aspect of how to understand the term "indigenous." He states that "'indigenous' labels the absence rather than the presence of a distinguishing characteristic."[9] The absence of what? The absence of possibilities, of equal access to resources, of valorization of their culture and religious outlook, and so forth. In this vein, the Kutchi Kohlis of Pakistan share the fate of the Quechuas of Peru or the Mayas of Guatemala. They too are between cultures, religions, and nation-states, possessing at the same time a particularity that deserves to be considered and seriously studied.

Taking these points into consideration, I am of the opinion that the term "indigenous" opens more possibilities for understanding and empowering the Kutchi Kohlis (Christians and Hindus). Even if the ethnological category "tribal" can be appropriate anthropologically, I think it is not sufficiently helpful for exploring and enhancing the spiritual experience of the Kutchi Kohlis.

## Definition of "Spirituality"

Defining spirituality can be a complex task, not only because there are multiple definitions available in academia but also because if a pluri-religious context such as Pakistan is considered, it is necessary to consider also the ways in which spirituality is perceived

---

8. Harvey, *Indigenous Religions*, 3–4.
9. Harvey, *Indigenous Religions*, 11.

*Introduction*

by individuals. In this sense, I think that a study of Kutchi Kohli Christian spirituality requires a definition of spirituality that (i) is not limited to a particular religious tradition, (ii) takes seriously the devotional and even supernatural, common understanding of a spiritual experience by some individuals, and (iii) dynamically takes into consideration the ongoing transformations of human spiritual experience.

In this perspective, Sandra Schneiders offers a definition of spirituality that covers the requirements of this research. Thus Schneiders states that spirituality is:

i. An existential phenomenon.[10]

ii. A way of living.[11]

She defines it as "the actualization of the basic human capacity for transcendence and . . . as the experience of conscious involvement in the project of life-integration through self-transcendence towards the horizon of ultimate value one perceives."[12] In addition, Philip Sheldrake considers that spirituality is not one element among others in the human condition but instead is an integrating dimension and refers to the search of meaning that can give sense to human life and experiences.[13] Furthermore, I think that Michael O'Sullivan's understanding of authenticity is pertinent for the study of Kutchi Kohli Christian spirituality. He understands authenticity as "the determined and sustained desire and commitment to reach what is really so and to act accordingly."[14] He adds that it is "a dynamic quality permeating our lived subjectivity and it guides us, foundationally and methodically towards contextualized beauty, truth, goodness, and love."[15]

---

10. Schneiders, "Approaches," 16.
11. Schneiders, "Approaches," 16.
12. Schneiders, "Approaches," 16.
13. Sheldrake, *Spirituality*, 8.
14. O'Sullivan, "'Authenticity,'" 2.
15. O'Sullivan, "'Authenticity,'" 2.

*Introduction*

Finally, I think it is important to consider the self-implicating character of the study of spirituality.[16] This is especially relevant in this research because I am part of the ethnic and religious community under study.

## Outline of the Chapters

I will briefly present in this section the different chapters of this research.

- Chapter 1 presents the pertinent literature on Kutchi Kohli Christians. It aims to point out their history, their main characteristics, and the ways in which they interact with other religious traditions. In addition, this chapter develops conceptual tools for analyzing Kutchi Kohli Christian Spirituality: interspirituality, multiple religious belonging, and hybridization.

- Chapter 2 includes the methodological framework of the research, highlighting the pertinence of using a qualitative methodology. Thus, the chapter includes a description of the narrative approach used for the in-depth interviews realized as part of this study. It also states the method used for analyzing the data provided by the interviews. The second part of the chapter develops the spirituality framework of the research. It points out in detail how spirituality is understood throughout the research as well as the use of "indigenous spirituality" as a conceptual framework for understanding Kutchi Kohli Christian spirituality.

- Chapter 3 focuses on presenting the findings of the six in-depth interviews realized as part of the research. It makes an analytical presentation of the findings and then groups them around common themes expressed by the participants.

- Chapter 4 offers an overview of the most important outcomes of this research. It also proposes some recommendations for empowering Kutchi Kohli Christians and fostering their

16. Frohlich, "Spiritual Discipline," 68.

*Introduction*

spiritual life. Finally, it states some conclusions and points out some areas for further research.

Considering the linguistic complexity of the study of Kutchi Kohlis, I have added a short glossary with some of the terms used in this book.

# 1

# Encountering and Understanding the Kutchi Kohli Christians

IN THIS CHAPTER I will present the object of the research, the Kutchi Kohli Christians, situating them in history and in their interaction to the larger Kutchi Kohli Hindu community and within the Islamic context of Pakistan. I will also describe the conceptual framework that will help me to analyze the spiritual experience of Kutchi Kohli Christians. In order to achieve this, I will present three concepts of analysis: (i) interspirituality, (ii) multiple or double religious belonging, and (iii) hybridization.

## The Kutchi Kohli Christian

### History of Catholic Kutchi Kohli Christians

Kutchi Kohli Christians are those, belonging to the larger Kutchi Kohli community of Pakistan, who accepted the faith in Jesus Christ that was brought to them through the activities of missionaries[1] who came to Sindh[2] to serve. According to the survey done

---

1. Although I will mostly refer to Catholic missionaries in this section, the term "missionaries," as well as the term "Kutchi Kohli Christians," refers to people belonging to different Christian denominations.

2. Sindh is the southern province of Pakistan.

## Exploring Indigenous Spirituality

by the first Kutchi Kohli priest, Fr. Mohan Victor, OFM, Catholic missionary activity among the Kutchi Kohlis was begun in 1943 by the Franciscan Friars in Nawabshah, a city of Sindh province.[3]

Those missionaries had to face challenges in understanding the characteristics of this population: religious, social, and ethnic structures, cultural features, and history. In those beginnings, the Kutchi Kohlis, as well as all the other indigenous groups in Pakistan, had been classified by a generic term "tribal people" since the time of the British occupation of what is nowadays Pakistan. The lack of information and knowledge of the languages meant that only progressively did the Franciscan friars discover that they were dealing not with one group but with many different indigenous groups besides Kutchi Kohli people. Thus, they began to learn from them, identify the boundaries between one group and another, and even recognize the difficulty of mixing people from one group with another. As a consequence of this, they concluded that indigenous groups of this area needed separate attention.[4] Thus the Catholic diocese of the area (Hyderabad) asked Franciscans to work with two groups of these indigenous people: the Kutchi Kohlis and the Parkari Kohlis. As Fr. Mohan states, "This was a diocesan decision and not just a Franciscan decision."[5] It was a solution due to reduced missionary personnel, transport difficulties, and the fact that many of these groups of people lived in distant and isolated areas. According to Master Mansingh Rawa, the Franciscans used to travel for many hours on bicycles in order to visit the Kutchi Kohli and Parkari Kohli communities.[6]

---

3. Victor, "General Survey," 1.
4. Victor, "General Survey," 1.
5. Victor, "General Survey," 1.
6. Rawa Mansingh, interview by Anita Mansingh on the history of Kutchi Kohli Christians, March 25, 2019.

## Encountering and Understanding the Kutchi Kohli Christians

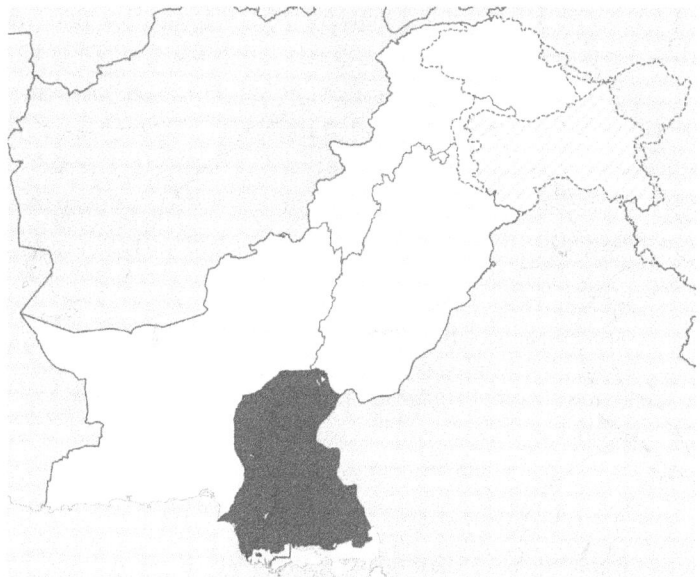

Map of Sindh Province, Pakistan.[7]

In contrast to the Parkari Kohli's reception of the mission in their community, the Kutchi Kohli people were reluctant and cautious about the activities of missionaries among them. For this reason, the Franciscan friars decided to work only with the Parkari Kohli community, except for one Franciscan, Fr. Firman, OFM, who continued working with the Kutchi Kohli people.[8] The situation remained like that for a number of years until the Mill Hill Missionaries came to the region in 1977. They decided to give special attention to the Kutchi Kohli people; among those missionaries were Frs. Brendan Mulhall, MHM, and Mark Connolly, MHM.[9] After working in Nawabshaw and Mirpur Khas, finally, a center for Kutchi Kohli Christians was opened in Tando Allahyar in 1986.[10]

---

7. "Sindh in Pakistan," Wikimedia Commons, https://commons.wikimedia.org/wiki/File:Sindh_in_Pakistan_(claims_hatched).svg.

8. Victor, "General Survey," 1.

9. Victor, "General Survey," 1.

10. Victor, "General Survey," 2. A hostel was opened in 1980 in Tando Allahyar under the responsibility of Master Mansingh.

Exploring Indigenous Spirituality

It would be in Tando Allahyar, and it is from there that Mill Hill Missionaries, Presentation Sisters, boarding school masters, and Masters (catechists) continue working for the empowerment of Kutchi Kohli Christians. At that time, Presentation Sisters Regina Coughlan and Emer Manning played a huge role in establishing educational facilities among Kutchi people as a means to open new possibilities for their future.

## Characteristics of Kutchi Kohli Christians

The characteristics of any group play a great role in the shaping of their spirituality. Like other indigenous people, the Kutchi Kohli Christians have some outstanding characteristics, such as the following.

- Hospitality is a leading mark of Kutchi Kohli culture. For Kutchi Kohli people their guest is welcomed as they would welcome God in their life. For Kutchi Kohli Christians this is strongly linked to Jesus's invitation, "Truly I tell you, whatever you did for one of the least of these brothers and sisters of mine, you did for me."[11]

- The reverence for the divine is heart-touching, as the Kutchi Kohli people do not enter any sacred place without removing their footwear; rather, they prefer to go barefoot. I will connect this idea of reverence for God, as a way of expressing their spirituality, with the passage in the book of Exodus: "'Do not come any closer,' God said. 'Take off your sandals, for the place where you are standing is holy ground.'"[12] This reverence for the sacred has been passed from generation to generation in the Kutchi Kohli people, whether they are Hindus or Christians. It shapes not only their attitude within a sacred space but also their relationship with nature, the land, and the divine present in creation.

---

11. Matt 25:40, NIV.
12. Exod 3:5, NIV.

- Emotions are strongly experienced and expressed. This aspect is important when the manners in which Kutchi Kohlis relate to others are studied. For instance, feelings of love and anger are strongly experienced and shape the behavior and choices of Kutchi Kohlis. However, it is important to mention that these strongly experienced feelings are in tension with a conservative environment in which love cannot be publicly expressed or anger must be hidden in order to respect, at least in appearance, the hierarchical social order. Furthermore, this also points to the importance of expression as a way of living: expression of feelings, desires, faith. Kutchi Kohlis are constantly seeking ways to express their emotions.

- Their spiritual experience has been shaped by multiple influences, including Hinduism and Islam, but also the fact that missionaries have brought with them their particular ways of understanding Christianity. Thus, the new generation of Catholic missionaries who came from the Philippines introduced ways to live and celebrate liturgy that contrasted with those encouraged by European Catholic missionaries.

## Living in an Islamic Context

To live in the Pakistani Islamic context has its own challenges for Kutchi Kohli Christians and Kutchi Kohli people in general for various reasons. Kutchi Kohli people are one of the minority[13] groups of Pakistan, and the current internal social, cultural, and religious tensions of the country, especially related to fundamentalism and intolerance, instill fear in their hearts because it is not always easy to express and practice their faith as they would wish to. An example would be an all-night Hindu devotional singing of hymns (*bhajans*) having to stop abruptly at the Muslim call to prayer, or the date of a major Kutchi Kohli festival—such as that of Rama Pir in Tando Allahyar—having to change if it fell during the

---

13. Here the term "minority" has multiple dimensions: ethnic minority, religious minority, cultural minority.

## Exploring Indigenous Spirituality

Muslim month of fasting, Ramadan. Feasts such as Christmas or Easter are celebrated in tension and with lots of security due to the possibility of extremist Muslims trying to stop the celebration by harming the people or creating terror through a bomb blast. The other example of living in fear for Kutchi Kohli Christians or other minority religions is that they are nervous and reticent to have a free conversation about religion because they are afraid they may be accused of blasphemy, as the recently released Asia Bibi was before suffering eight long years of solitary confinement in jail. Furthermore, this experience of fear has as its consequence "internalized oppression," which remains deeply present in the lives of Christians. Thus, Fr. John O'Brien, CSSp, states that

> while the Christian minority is systematically and structurally oppressed, the chronic dysfunctionality in the immediate and intermediate terms, results from the internalization of this oppression and the replication of destructive behavior patterns of revenge, exclusion and *mepris* within the community itself.[14]

This internalized oppression is an aspect which needs to be dealt with in order to shape a healthy and free spirituality for the empowerment of Kutchi Kohli Christians.

However, not all can be considered negative or destructive in this relationship between Kutchi Kohlis (Christians or Hindus) and Muslims. Thus, another important aspect to highlight is the fact that Christians, Hindus, and Muslims share sacred spaces and some devotional practices at some of the shrines in Sindh. For instance, the mausoleum of Shah Abdul Latif Bhittai is a Muslim shrine where every year many Kutchi Kohli people visit at the festival or *urs* of this saint. I remember that my grandfather faithfully used to go there every year, and a few times I also visited that shrine with him. Other shrines are also shared by Muslim and Kutchi Kohli people, such as the shrines of Lal Shahbaz Qalandar and Odero Lal. In addition, it is also important to notice that Kutchi Kohli Christians are adopting the language and vocabulary used by Muslims.

---

14. O'Brien, *Hope That Is Still with Us*, 116.

For instance, Kutchi Kohli Christians use *Isu Ni Jai*[15] as a greeting expression, but in interaction with Muslims they use *Assalam-o Alaikum*.[16] Or take the term *eid*, which, although being an Islamic term, is commonly used to refer to Christian feasts also. Finally, it is important to mention the impact that education—especially the way in which history is studied at schools, highlighting the centrality of Islam—has upon the identity of Kutchi Kohlis.

It is important to point out that the impact of the Islamic ethos of Pakistan is different among different Christian communities in Pakistan. For instance, the Muslim practices of Ramadan, the Muslim period of fasting, are shaping the way in which Punjabi Christians practice fasting during the liturgical season of Lent. Thus, there is an increasing practice of a total fasting during daylight and the introduction of a prayer time for breaking the fast of the day. This cannot be observed among Kutchi Kohlis, who prefer fasting by limiting their consumption of food to fruit and water.

## Hindu Influence

The influence of Hinduism upon Kutchi Kohli Christians is pervasive and cannot be either underestimated or considered an external influence. The fact that usually only a small family unit converts to Christianity while the extended family remains Hindu produces a complex interaction between Kutchi Kohli Christians and Kutchi Kohli Hindus. For instance, my father with his siblings was educated by the Franciscan friars living in a boarding school, so they were baptized and became Christian, while my grandfather remained Hindu. In his later life, he was living with us in my father's house, where I experienced Christian and Hindu practices. Thus, my father kept his Catholic faith practices while my grandfather had his own sacred place in his room where he worshiped Hindu gods and goddess. In a similar way, there are some feasts of Hinduism which are still being celebrated by Kutchi

---

15. This expression is in the Kutchi Kohli language.
16. This expression is in Arabic and Urdu.

Kohlis in Pakistan, such as Diwali (feast of light), Holi or Houtani (the spring feast), and Hachmon (the feast to remember the return of lord Shiva from exile in which sweet food is cooked).[17] It is particularly interesting in the case of Diwali, the "biggest feast of the Kutchi year."[18] Even though all the Kutchis are not aware of the meaning behind this feast, they do believe that its purpose is the overcoming of darkness by lighting candles and lamps (*divas*). Furthermore, this feast is an invitation to reconciliation. If relatives are angry with each other, on this feast they ask pardon and are reunited with each other.[19] Among Kutchi Christians, this feast has been Christianized to explain to people that Christ is the "Light of the world." This is part of "the process of creating new Christian forms from the culture in which missionaries find themselves."[20]

Another important influence of Hinduism upon Kutchi Kohli Christians is the feast of Rama Pir, who is an important holy man for the Kutchi Kohli Hindus. Every year many Kutchi Kohlis visit the temple of Rama Pir on his feast day in autumn. His temple situated in Tando Allahyar is very famous among Hindus of the subcontinent.[21] This feast shapes the life of Kutchi Kohli Christians in multiple ways. Firstly, it is a way to express their devotion, to cope with their emotions (sufferings, pain, joys, and so forth). Secondly, it is also a time of deep personal prayer and encounter with the divine that shapes Kutchi Kohli Christians' spirituality. This is in line with the perspective of S. Wesley Ariarajah, who states that "each person is called to express spiritual life in a particular way which is appropriate to one's nature and place in human life."[22] Finally, it is a space of interaction between Christian and Hindu Kutchi Kohlis.

The influence of Hinduism permeates all the dimensions of the life of the Kutchi Kohli Christians. Thus, in the wedding ceremony, a particular rite called *fera* (moving in a circle around the

---

17. Mulhall, "Kutchi Kohlis of Sindh," 55.
18. Mulhall, "Kutchi Kohlis of Sindh," 54.
19. Mulhall, "Kutchi Kohlis of Sindh," 54.
20. Teasdale, *Mystic Heart*, 37.
21. Mulhall, "Kutchi Kohlis of Sindh," 56.
22. Ariarajah, "Hindu Spirituality," 78.

fire) is performed. This ritual is still being practiced by the Kutchi Kohli Christians for various reasons: First, it keeps the family and social bond with the larger Hindu community and relatives who are Hindus intact. Second, the symbols used in this ritual are full of meaning for the Kutchi Kohli community, and the ritual itself expresses the union between man and woman. In addition to the value of keeping this practice, the ritual of moving in a circle remains, but it has been Christianized in that the fire or a candle put in the middle of the circle represents the light of Christ, and a crucifix and a Bible are placed beside it. In addition, if a Catholic priest is available, he celebrates a liturgy of the word as well as the ritual imparting of a blessing on the couple.

## Complementary Conceptual Tools of Analysis

In order to fully understand the spiritual experience of the Kutchi Kohli Christians, it is necessary to have conceptual tools that assist us to understand it. Firstly, I will explore the ways in which Kutchi Kohli Christians interact with their Hindu background as well as with the Islamic context of Pakistan. Secondly, I will examine the manner in which these concepts may help us to understand how such interactions play a role in the construction of the Kutchi Kohli Christian identity. Finally, these conceptual tools may help us identify aspects within the Kutchi Kohli spiritual life that can help Kutchi Kohli Christians deepen their experience of God and empower them for facing the challenges of the Pakistani context. Consequently, I will use the concepts of interspirituality, multiple or double religious belonging, and hybridization. Before proceeding to explain these concepts, I would like to situate graphically these multiple interactions.

## Exploring Indigenous Spirituality

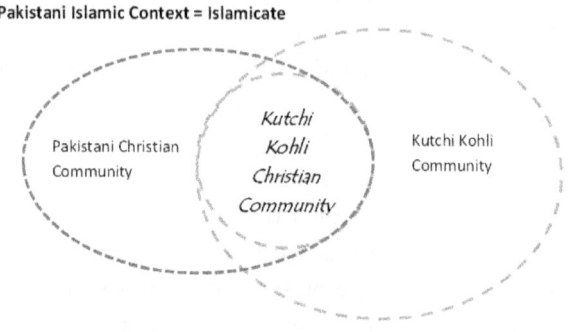

Kutchi Kohli Christians in the Pakistani Islamic Context.

## Interspirituality

Interspirituality is an important and useful tool for understanding the spirituality of another person in all its complexity, especially in those cases in which some of the elements of the spiritual life of a person belong to multiple religious and spiritual traditions. Furthermore, this concept allows a non-judgmental approach to the complexity and diversity of the human religious experience, opening the researcher to the possibility of identifying the value and dynamics of the religious, spiritual, and mystical experience of a person or community. In this perspective, interspirituality does not refer to external elements incorporated into the spiritual experience of a people (individuals or community), neither to a distortion of a pure original spiritual experience; instead, as Wayne Teasdale states, "the prefix '*inter*' in interspirituality expresses the ontological roots that tie the various traditions together and that are responsible for religions influencing each other throughout history."[23] Furthermore, he says that "'*inter*' means an openness to learn from others, and the wisdom of their traditions; it is a trust in what will be found; it is the conscious assimilation of whatever is valuable to

---

23. Teasdale, *Mystic Heart*, 27.

aid one's own journey."[24] Thus, this concept refers to a constitutive characteristic of the spiritual experience, and it is in this perspective that I will use this concept for analyzing the spiritual experience of the Kutchi Kohli Christians. In addition, interspirituality as a tool of understanding provides a wider comprehension of what spirituality is, observing it as a dynamic and porous phenomenon rather than a model of study whose boundary would be limited by a particular religious tradition. Moreover, interspirituality makes it possible to study the personal freedom dynamic of an individual in search of a mystical experience which can be facilitated by elements coming from any religious tradition or spiritual practice that speaks to one's heart. For Celia Kourie, "The essence of the interspiritual path is the phenomenon of mysticism."[25]

In this perspective, it is important to state that "interspirituality is not a one-way street, but an intermystical interaction where insights cross back and forth, intermingle, and find new habitats."[26] It helps us to recognize that "there are multiple dimensions and expressions of the sacred"[27] which can be experienced in the diversity of traditions, cultures, and religions. In addition, this conceptual tool will help us to understand the nature and characteristics of the possible bond between the spiritual experiences arising from different religious traditions—in the case of this research, between Christianity, Hinduism, and Islam. However, it is important to note that the idea of interspirituality did not gain favor from some scholars of religion who are involved in inter-faith dialogue.[28] The reason for not accepting the concept of interspirituality is its "liberal assumptions that are unsettling for more committed religious persons [e.g., conservative evangelicals]."[29] I think that it is important to be aware of this tension between belonging/commitment within a particular religious tradition and a more complex internal,

---

24. Teasdale, *Mystic Heart*, 27.
25. Kourie, "Crossing Boundaries," 20.
26. Teasdale, *Mystic Heart*, 27.
27. Kourie, "Crossing Boundaries," 16.
28. Kourie, "Crossing Boundaries," 21.
29. Kourie, "Crossing Boundaries," 21.

although social, spiritual experience, without considering them as opposite dynamics. Instead, in my opinion, keeping in mind both aspects can lead to a deep understanding of the spiritual life of a person. Thus, understanding the dynamics of interspirituality can help to identify some spiritual elements that attract people of different cultural traditions and religions together and provide a more inclusive lens for studying spirituality and people's spiritual journey in their search for reaching the divine.

## Multiple/Double Religious Belonging

Multiple/double religious belonging as a concept and reality can provide a fruitful and adequate way for understanding the spiritual experiences of the Kutchi Kohli Christians. As Catherine Cornille states, multiple or double religious belonging is a phenomenon present for centuries in Asia, in contrast to the West where religious categories and belonging have had more rigid and exclusive boundaries in the past.[30] Thus, in order to understand the internal dynamics of the spiritual life of the Kutchi Kohli Christians, it is important to be conscious that this Asian reality of multiple or double religious belonging "bypasses the very purpose and dynamics of religious belonging."[31] Furthermore,

> double or multiple religious belonging implies a certain holding back, an inability to fully accept some form of heteronomy, or an inability to let go of one religion when in heart and mind one has already converted to another.[32]

This has as a consequence that "double [multiple] religious belonging may thus manifest itself in the form of belonging to the symbolic and historical framework of one religion and the hermeneutical framework of another."[33]

---

30. Cornille, "Double Religious Belonging," 43.
31. Cornille, "Double Religious Belonging," 48.
32. Cornille, "Double Religious Belonging," 49.
33. Cornille, "Double Religious Belonging," 47.

At the theological level, the concept of multiple or double religious belonging opens a person to the possibility to accept that all the religions lead to the same destiny, which is God. As Claude Geffré states,

> We are witnessing much greater optimism about the possibility of salvation from within the other religions of the world, and we have gone beyond a conception of mission oriented in the first place to "conversion," understood as the change of religion.[34]

For instance, in an earlier time, it was assumed by the missionaries that conversion meant changing the religion of the people to make them Christian because it was thought that there was no salvation outside the Catholic Church. In a similar way, many Muslims consider that there is no other way to reach God or to find salvation except through Islam. This point is important in the framework of our research because a sound and healthy Kutchi Kohli Christian spirituality may give positive ground for answering the question about the salvation of others, the Kutchi Kohli Christians being, in themselves, a small minority.

From this point of view, it would be necessary to consider that "being or becoming" a Christian is not only about changing some cultural or spiritual values of an indigenous people, but it is also about changing the way of being Christian by adopting the traditions and perspectives of indigenous peoples. Claude Geffré quotes Cardinal Malula, Archbishop of Kinshasa, who used to say, "So far, we have Christianized Africa, it is now time to Africanize Christianity."[35] In this perspective, analyzing the dynamics of multiple belonging can make it possible:

- to explore the ways in which Kutchi Kohli Christians make sense of this multiplicity of belongings at the spiritual level, without considering their experiences or practices impure or inferior to other forms of Christian spirituality.

---

34. Geffré, "Double Belonging," 93.
35. Geffré, "Double Belonging," 97.

Exploring Indigenous Spirituality

- to consider Kutchi Kohli Christians as "liminal figures" because the research will deal with first-, second-, and third-generation Christians who belong to extended Hindu families living in an Islamic context.

- to identify ways to enhance and empower Kutchi Kohli Christian spiritual experiences without separating them from their roots, rituals, and traditions that can allow them to have a deep relationship with the divine.

Thus, "the question remains open as to whether it is possible to imagine a Christian identity that would also integrate the positive values of another great non-Christian tradition."[36]

## Hybridization

The third tool which can help understand Kutchi Kohli Christian spirituality is hybridization. This concept allows exploring how the broader context, what in Figure 2 has been denominated "Islamic context," or "Islamicate,"[37] has an impact on other cultures and religious identities living in the same territory. This can be shaping them, enhancing them, calling them into question, or even destroying them. Thus, "hybridization's concern is with interactions, negotiations, and mutual enrichment among these cultures."[38] In addition, Friedman points out that "the concept of hybridization posits then that cultures are neither given nor fixed; rather they flow and tend to blend."[39] Thus, with the passage of time and generations, things kept changing as well as cultures. Cultures change not only through internal processes of transformation but also when they adopt something from a different culture, either

---

36. Geffré, "Double Belonging," 98.

37. The term "Islamicate" refers to the broader cultural environment produced by a Muslim society in which non-Muslim cultures develop in dialogue with and influenced by the larger conceptual and symbolic framework. See Hodgson, *Classical Age of Islam*.

38. Shimoni and Bergmann, "Managing in a Changing World," 78.

39. Shimoni, "Cultural Borders," 219.

consciously or unconsciously. They also change when they let go of some practices that have been performed during generations and start processes of mixing with other culture. It is this dynamic process of interaction and transformation that denotes hybridization.

It is also important to highlight that "hybridization," in contrast to the idea of "syncretism," does not imply the existence of a "pure condition" in a religion or cultural tradition. Hybridization implies seeing cultures and religions, as dynamic, and even more to consider this dynamism "as the ongoing condition of all human cultures, which contains no zone of purity."[40] As a consequence of this approach, it is possible to assess the incorporation of religious and cultural practices of one culture into another, but not as a process of degeneration or contamination; instead it can be considered from the perspective of the internal dynamism of a culture and/or religion.

However, it is important to mention that the hybridization process can also be understood as a negative consequence of interaction with a more powerful or dominant culture or religion. Thus, Homi K. Bhabha considers that "hybridization is the process by which the colonial power tries to shape the identity of the colonized within a homogeneous framework, but then fails, producing something familiar but new."[41] I do not think there is a need to choose between dimensions of the process of hybridization, especially while studying the Kutchi Kohlis Christians. Both movements of enrichment and transformation, as well as homogenization and disarticulation, can be identified as present among the Kutchi Kohlis in their relation with the larger Islamic context of Pakistan. Nevertheless, this concept helps us to recognize that:

i. the Kutchi Kohli interaction with Islam is not, at least not always, a relation of contamination and distortion of the Kutchi Kohli identity.[42]

---

40. Shimoni, "Cultural Borders," 219.

41. See Shimoni and Bergmann, "Managing in a Changing World," 78.

42. This point is also valid for the relationship with Christianity and Christians from different cultural backgrounds.

ii. the Kutchi Kohli Christian spirituality may be studied in its complex relationship with Islam and Islamic spirituality.

## Summary

The aim of this chapter was to introduce the object of the research, the Kutchi Kohli Christians, their historical context, and their interactions with others. It has been shown that the research is dealing with first-, second-, and third-generation Christians who belong to an indigenous group of Pakistan: the Kutchi Kohlis. I have argued that the term "indigenous" is adequate for referring to the Kutchi Kohlis and can help to consider their spiritual experience not as a distortion of any world religion, but as a particular and meaningful way to relate to the divine and to others. I have also pointed out that in order to properly understand the spiritual experience of the Kutchi Kohli Christians it is necessary to study it in their interaction with the larger Kutchi Kohli Hindu community. Thus, the Hindu background of the Kutchi Kohli Christians must not be considered as an obstacle for a Christian experience; instead it may be understood as the ground in which the Christian faith may be rooted and as a symbolic and conceptual well from which Kutchi Kohli Christians will draw symbols and ways to relate to the divine that can enhance their spiritual experience. In order to achieve this, I have posited a conceptual framework of analysis that involves considering the spiritual experiences of Kutchi Kohlis from a threefold perspective: (i) interspirituality, (ii) multiple religious belonging, and (iii) hybridization.

## 2

# A Narrative Approach to the Spiritual Life of the Kutchi Kohli Christians

IN THIS CHAPTER, I will present the methodology that will be used for the research. I will do this at two levels. I will first present the approach and method that I will use for the fieldwork and for analyzing the data collected. Then, at a second level, I will present the methodological considerations for studying the spiritual experience of the Kutchi Kohli Christians.

## Methodology Framework

### Qualitative Methodology

There are different theoretical methodologies for studying spirituality. In order to achieve the aim of my research, I will use a qualitative methodology for studying the spirituality of Kutchi Kohli people during the fieldwork and data analysis. According to Steven J. Taylor, Robert Bogdan, and Marjorie L. DeVault, "The phrase qualitative methodology refers in the broadest sense to research that produces descriptive data—people's own written or spoken words and observable behavior."[1] The qualitative methodology al-

---

1. Taylor et al., *Introduction to Qualitative Research*, 21.

lows the researcher to focus on the experiences of the people and the meanings they find in their lives.² Furthermore, qualitative methodology opens the way towards learning and understanding "concepts such as beauty, pain, faith, suffering, frustration, and love whose essence is lost through other research approaches."³ This will allow me to approach the interiority of the spiritual experience of Kutchi Kohli Christians. Similarly, the qualitative methodology allows the researcher to study people from every aspect, such as their past and present or even their future in any situation where people are found.⁴ Thus, the emphasis of qualitative methodology is on the process of producing meaning.⁵ The qualitative methodology allows the "researchers to develop concepts, insights, and understandings from patterns in the data rather than collecting data to assess preconceived models, hypotheses, or theories."⁶ I consider this essential for exploring a spiritual experience; for instance, in the case of Kutchi Kohlis Christians there are many preconceived ideas about their spiritual life (syncretic, underdeveloped, superficial, and so forth), and the data can be used for confirming some of these ideas, or the data can be used for exploring how Kutchi Kohli Christians experienced, articulated, and expressed their spiritual life.

## The Narrative Approach

The use of the "narrative approach" will allow me to explore the process of construction of meaning and identity among the Kutchi Kohli Christians at the level of their spiritual life. This approach "takes as a premise that people live and/or understand their lives in storied forms, connecting events in the manner of a plot that

2. Taylor et al., *Introduction to Qualitative Research*.
3. Taylor et al., *Introduction to Qualitative Research*, 23.
4. Taylor et al., *Introduction to Qualitative Research*.
5. Taylor et al., *Introduction to Qualitative Research*, 24.
6. Taylor et al., *Introduction to Qualitative Research*, 22.

has a beginning, middle, and end point."[7] This narrative character of any human experience is essential for my research for two reasons. First, it is the appropriate way to approach a culture in which wisdom, as well as history, is primarily communicated orally to this day; thus, it is through this oral character of the Kutchi Kohlis of Pakistan that I plan to study their spiritual life. Secondly, I think that in order to have an in-depth understanding of the complexity of the spiritual experience of an indigenous people such as the Kutchi Kohlis, it is necessary to allow them to narrate their experience of God in order to make sense of and give meaning to their external practices and interior experiences. In this perspective, narrative research makes it possible to explore how Kutchi Kohlis give meaning to their spiritual experiences, articulating them and introducing them in a continuum.[8] In this context, it is important to point out that in this kind of approach the researcher is not dealing, necessarily, with "factual" events, but with the manner in which these events are experienced and interpreted by the agents themselves.[9] Furthermore, the narrative approach is "an interpretative enterprise consisting of the joint subjectivities of researcher and participants";[10] this point is particularly relevant because of my personal implication in this topic, I myself being a Kutchi Kohli Christian. Thus, it will be important to be attentive to the auto-ethnographical dimension throughout this research.

In the same line, the work of Paul Ricoeur will deepen our narrative approach to the Kutchi Kohli spiritual experience. Ricoeur underscores and privileges the reflective character of narrative in the constitution of personal or communitarian identity.[11] Thus, the narrative theory of Paul Ricoeur applied to the construction of the self (interiority and exteriority) will be an essential aspect for understanding Kutchi Kohli Christian spirituality in its movement from Hinduism to Christianity.

7. Wertz et al., *Doing Qualitative Analysis*, 224.
8. Wertz et al., *Doing Qualitative Analysis*.
9. Wertz et al., *Doing Qualitative Analysis*, 225.
10. Wertz et al., *Doing Qualitative Analysis*.
11. Ricoeur, *Time and Narrative*; Ricoeur, *Oneself as Another*.

Exploring Indigenous Spirituality

## In-Depth Interview

In order to collect the data needed for the study, I will proceed with in-depth interviews with a selected number of persons in order to explore their spiritual experience. By in-depth interviewing I mean to encounter people face to face in order to understand their "perspectives on their lives, experiences, or situations as expressed in their own words."[12] As Seidman suggests, the in-depth interview allows exploring the different dynamics of the lived experiences of Kutchi Kohli people.[13] Furthermore, the in-depth interview makes it possible to identify how Kutchi Kohli people give meaning to their spiritual experiences. It is important to mention that I will proceed with an open-ended and semi-structured interview during the process of data collection.

## Method of Analyzing Data

I will use NVivo 12 Plus as software for analyzing the data collected through the in-depth interviews. NVivo allows the researcher to manage data and ideas, query and visualize the data, and report the data;[14] this makes it possible not only to organize the data thematically but also to have quick access to the information scattered throughout the interviews. Thus, the software will help me to analyze and interpret the spiritual experience of those Kutchi Kohli Christians interviewed.

I will use the software following some of the steps pointed out by Al Yahmadi Hamed Hilal and Saleh Said Alabri.[15] Thus, the process will be as described in the following figure:

---

12. Taylor et al., *Introduction to Qualitative Research*, 102.
13. Taylor et al., *Introduction to Qualitative Research*.
14. Bazeley and Jackson, *Qualitative Data Analysis*, 3.
15. Hilal and Alabri, "Using NVivo for Data Analysis," 182.

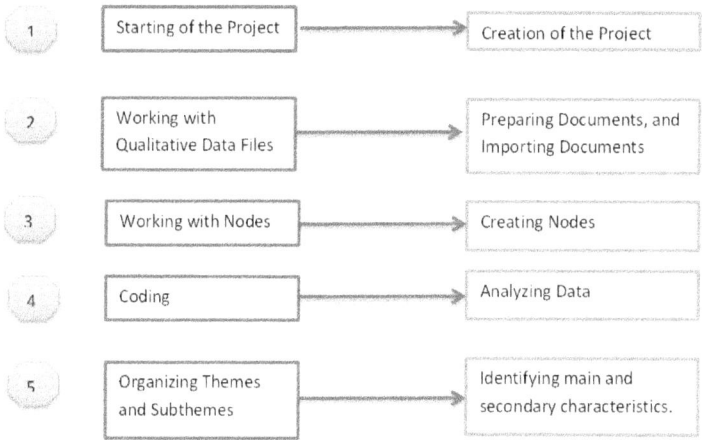

**Process of Data Analysis with NVivo**

It is this categorization of the data that is central for the success of the research. In this sense, I will proceed to the analysis in a dialectical way, underscoring first the data expressed by the interview and then contrasting this with the conceptual tools described in the preceding chapter.

## Spirituality Framework

### Towards a Complex Understanding of Spirituality

At the first and general level and in order to study Kutchi Kohli Christian Spirituality, it is necessary to have a complex understanding of spirituality that allows us to consider how the multiple elements are present in the sociocultural and spiritual context in which Kutchi Kohli Christians live and shape their spiritual experience, but also how they are not passive; instead they are creative actors of their own spiritual experience.

In this perspective, Sandra Schneiders's definition of spirituality makes it possible to situate the research at the level of the human experience, instead of focusing on how belonging to a particular religious tradition shapes the spiritual life of a person or group.¹⁶ Thus, Schneiders understands spirituality as "the actualization of the human capacity for transcendence... as the experience of conscious involvement in the project of life-integration through self-transcendence toward the horizon of ultimate value one perceives."¹⁷ Firstly, this definition of spirituality allows the research to be focused on how Kutchi Kohli Christians actualize this human capacity, instead of asking how they conform their spiritual life to the tradition of the church. Second, this definition leads the researcher to wonder about the kind of awareness that Kutchi Kohli Christians have of their spiritual life as shaping and/or contributing to the building of a particular project of life. On this point, it is important to note that in South Asia we cannot understand this awareness purely as a subjective phenomenon; instead, it must be understood as an intersubjective experience. As Ayesha Jalal suggests, in South Asia it is important to consider the permanent "search for a balance between the will of the individual and a collective ethos."¹⁸ In her study of Muslim¹⁹ identity in South Asia²⁰ she underlines the need to consider the different "conceptions of *khudi* or self, and the related concept of self-determination or *khudikhtiyari*, in [the] collective assertion of sovereignty."²¹ Thus, to explore Kutchi Kohli Christian spirituality is to enter into the ways in which Kutchi Kohli Christians shape their own selves, subjectively and intersubjectively as in a constant dialogue between oneself and the others, between a collectivistic and individualistic culture. Finally, Schneiders's definition of spirituality points out the directionality of the spiritual experience, a key element in order to study a group like the Kutchi Kohli Christians,

16. Schneiders, "Spirituality in the Academy," 682.
17. Schneiders, "Approaches to the Study," 16.
18. Jalal, *Self and Sovereignty*, 12.
19. Ayesha Jalal also considers, even if briefly, the process in the Hindu community in present-day Pakistan. See Jalal, *Self and Sovereignty*, 436–41.
20. Although Ayesha Jalal is studying the construction of the Muslim political identity in South Asia, I think her considerations are valid for exploring the construction of the spiritual identity in this region.
21. Jalal, *Self and Sovereignty*, 12. The term used for "self" in the Kutchi Kohli language is *potay*.

who relatively recently became Christians. Thus, it must be considered how their spiritual experience is the result of having discovered and appropriated a new horizon of values as pertinent for their lives. In this framework, this research attempts to explore the human interiority of Kutchi Kohli Christians as Mary Frohlich suggested.[22] In addition, Frohlich's considerations highlighted the importance of focusing on "lived spirituality";[23] this implies a consideration of Kutchi Kohli Christian spirituality not only as a subjective/intersubjective reality but also as a changing reality in constant interaction with its cultural, social, and religious environment.

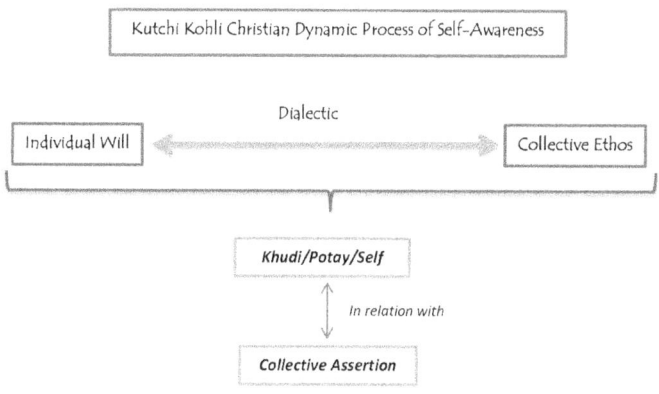

**Kutchi Kohli Christian Dynamic of Self-Awareness.**

## Indigenous Spirituality as a Conceptual Framework of Understanding

The second level of the spirituality framework of this research focuses on the Kutchi Kohli spirituality from the perspective of the category "indigenous." Having explored in the preceding chapters the pertinence of using the term "indigenous" for referring to the Kutchi Kohlis, I will focus in this section on two common features

22. Frohlich, "Spiritual Discipline," 76.
23. Frohlich, "Spiritual Discipline," 68.

of indigenous peoples' spirituality and their pertinence for studying Kutchi Kohli Christian spirituality, and then on the dialectic between Kutchi Kohli Christian spirituality and their belonging to the Kutchi Kohli indigenous people.

Ann Marie B. Bahr points out two key aspects, among others, for studying indigenous peoples: first, their resistance/resilience to being assimilated by conquerors or dominant cultures or powers, and second, that although many of them have been converted to one of the major world religions they have colored and transformed these traditions from within.[24] Michael O'Sullivan's concept of "authenticity" can help us to deepen the first dynamic as a factor shaping Kutchi Kohli Christian spirituality. He states that "authenticity" is "the determined and sustained desire and commitment to reach what is really so and to act accordingly."[25] Thus, O'Sullivan links the internal experience with the external action ("act accordingly") as an essential characteristic for understanding spiritual life. In a context of religious and social discrimination it is central to explore:

i. how the spiritual experience of the Kutchi Kohli Christians shapes their action and their relation to the context in which they live.

ii. how the perspective of an internal and external harmony/coherence ("authenticity") in the spiritual life can help to identify the ways in which Kutchi Kohli people deal with internalized oppression as described by John O'Brien.[26] This considering the possibility that a wounded identity,[27] as a

24. Bahr, *Indigenous Religions*, 6.

25. O'Sullivan, "'Authenticity,'" 6.

26. As stated in the preceding chapter, the structural marginalization, discrimination, and violence against Christians has produced an internalized oppression that needs to be healed not only from a social and psychological perspective, but also from a perspective that considers the spiritual dimension of this oppression. In my opinion this is a key aspect for empowering Kutchi Kohli Christians. See O'Brien, *Hope That Is Still with Us*, 115–18.

27. John O'Brien develops this idea in his study of the Punjabi Pakistani Christians. I think that it can be applied by extension as a tool of interpretation to the Kutchi Kohli Christian identity too. However, it is important to remember that Kutchi Kohli Christians and Punjabi Christians hold different positions

result of this context, needs to be healed in the process of empowering Kutchi Kohli Christians.²⁸

In addition, the conceptual tools described in the preceding chapter (multiple religious belonging and hybridization) will help to understand spirituality in constant interaction with other religious and cultural traditions.²⁹

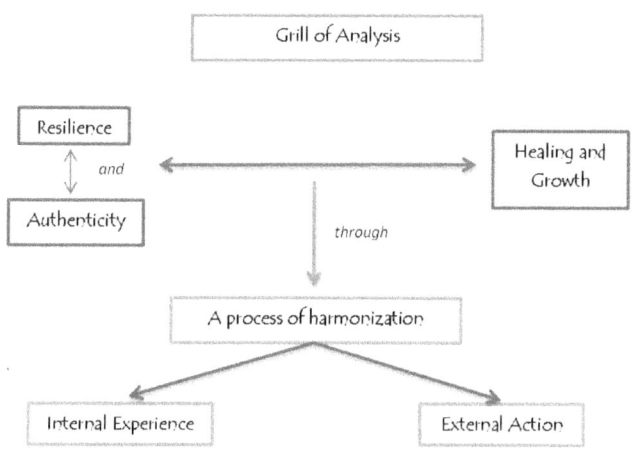

**Authenticity and Resilience as a Grill of Analysis.**

Finally, I would like to point out the importance of understanding Kutchi Kohli Christian spirituality as a dialectic understanding between their being Christian and their being Kutchi Kohlis. It will not be possible to talk about or even suggest ways of empowering

---

(sometimes considered insiders or outsiders by scholars) within and in relation to the Hindu caste system. See O'Brien, *The Unconquered People*, 1–46.2012

28. John O'Brien has depicted the process of shaping a new identity among the Punjabi Christians of Pakistan. However, his research does not focus on the spiritual dimension of their lives; instead he follows a more socio-anthropological approach. Furthermore, O'Brien in this context does not dwell on the case of members of indigenous communities who have over the last sixty years or more become Christian. Nevertheless, his considerations are an insightful source for understanding the internal dynamics of Pakistani Christians in general. See O'Brien, *Pakistani Christian Identity*, 547–616.

29. I developed these concepts in the preceding chapter.

## Exploring Indigenous Spirituality

them if we do not consider the ways in which they relate to their *Kutchikohliness*.[30] This is in the perspective of O'Sullivan's understanding of authenticity as "a dynamic quality permeating our lived subjectivity." Consequently, it would be necessary to explore:

i. how they relate to their *Kutchikohliness*.

ii. how this relation shapes their relationships with other Christians (Punjabi Pakistani Christians and missionaries from other countries).

iii. how this relation shapes their interaction with Muslims and Hindus, and especially with Kutchi Kohli Hindus.

This structure comes from considering Frederick Barth's idea that in order to understand the human experience of an ethnic group we need to focus on what happened within its boundaries.[31] It is in this porous boundary that Kutchi Kohli Christian spiritual and social identity is in the making.

Shaping an Identity: From Destructive to Creative Tension

**Identity Relation of Kutchi Kohli Christians with Their *Kutchikohliness***

---

30. I created this neologism in order to name the cultural, social, and religious substratum at the heart of the spiritual and social life of Kutchi Kohli Christians.

31. Against an essentialist understanding of ethnic groups, Barth suggests to focus on the boundaries between one and other as the place in which identity is formed and reformed constantly in a process of negotiation with the other. See Barth, *Ethnic Groups and Boundaries*, 9–38.

# 3

# Kutchi Kohli Voices and the Shaping of Their Identity

IN THIS CHAPTER, I will proceed to present the findings of the in-depth interviews conducted among Kutchi Kohli Christians.[1] The thematic division has as its objective to organize the information in a way that respects the voice of the interviewed[2] and at the same time represents a systematization of the information. As part of this analysis, I will also make analytic use of the conceptual tools described in the preceding chapters while considering the data of the interviews. I think it is important to mention that being myself a Kutchi Kohli Christian, the transcript of the interviews must be also considered in their meta-textual level; the participants have made allusions to events, persons, or cultural details, assuming

---

1. For confidentiality I am not using the real names of those interviewed. However, I decided to assign a proper name to them instead of using a number or letter. This is in order to respect their identity; this is particularly important considering that the Kutchi Kohlis have been oppressed and excluded.

2. It is important to mention that the interviews were conducted in the Urdu and Kutchi Kohli languages; thus here I am presenting my personal translation. In many cases and in order to respect the voice of the participants, I did not change the grammatical construction of the phrases, neither the metaphors used by the interviewed. I am conscious that some of them may sound strange to native English speakers, but as language conveys meaning, these particular structures and metaphors do too.

## Kutchi Kohli Christian Identity and *Kutchikohliness*

A first area in which the findings of the interviews can be systematized is the way in which Kutchi Kohli Christians relate to their Kutchi Kohli identity[3]—what in the spiritual framework I have denominated as *Kutchikohliness*.[4] Thus, during the interviews, the participants have described themselves as Christians and Kutchi Kohlis, highlighting sometimes the weight and newness of their Christian identity and other times the richness of their *Kutchikohliness*. In addition, the tension that can arise between these two belongings has been pointed out,[5] showing the dialectic of continuity and discontinuity at the identity level.[6]

### Identity and Self-Perception

A first aspect that needs to be highlighted is that the participants clearly perceive themselves as being Christians, and this self-perception reveals itself as constitutive of their social, religious, and spiritual identity. It is this self-awareness that leads them to perceive their religious identity and spiritual life either in continuity or in discontinuity with their *Kutchikohliness*.

Thus, Prem, while affirming his Christian identity, highlights the discontinuity with the past as he stated, "I am a born Christian. We have said goodbye to the religion of our ancestors and accepted Christianity and now it is in our blood. Now we are called people

---

3. I refer to their belongingness to the Kutchi Kohli community as an ethnic, social, cultural, and religious community.

4. Cf. chapter 1, section "Complementary Conceptual Tools of Analysis."

5. In chapter 1, I have developed the idea of multiple religious belonging as a conceptual tool for understanding some of the spiritual dynamics of the Kutchi Kohli Christians. Cf. Cornille, *Many Mansions?*

6. Paul Ricoeur describes this dialectic in his narrative theory. Ricoeur, *Time and Narrative*.

of the Bible." In the same vein, Mohan said, "I am 100 percent Christian and there is neither influence nor involvement of other religions' activities in my life." In another level of discontinuity, while referring to his Christian identity, Aakash mentions the emergence of a new social setting among Kutchi Kohlis, especially those who are Christians; he points out that because there is no more *biradheri* system,[7] people are now able to deal with their family issues for themselves. In this perspective, he suggests a new social setting and states that "our Kutchi Kohli community, they are strong in their faith and it is visible, and they are spending their lives on what Jesus preached." It is important to notice that although pointing out discontinuity, Aakash does not use the adjective "Christian" for referring to his community; instead, he uses the possessive "our" as denoting the particularity of his community of belonging.

On the other hand, Sohana sees her identity as different but related to her *Kutchikohliness*: "I am a Kutchi Kohli Christian." For her, there is no need to separate herself from her *Kutchikohliness* in order to be a Christian.

At the level of the perception of the Kutchi Kohli Christian community, the participants agree on highlighting the particularity of the Christian community, but at the same time, they are able to point out the goodness coming from and present in the larger Kutchi Kohli community. Thus, they agree on the self-perception that Kutchi Kohlis are hospitable, loving, tolerant, and ready to forgive and help others.[8] In addition, they point out some special characteristics of the Kutchi Kohli Christian community. Thus,

---

7. O'Brien in his study of the Punjabi Christian considers that "the ethnic identity has been guarded by the *biradheri* and within the *biradheri*, people found shelter from hostility. Allegiance was paramount: the *biradheri* defined duties, rights, loyalties, priorities and behavior." He also mentions the lack of an appropriate translation of this term, suggesting using it without translating. O'Brien, *Pakistani Christian Identity*, 628.

8. Prem, Mohan, Sonia, Maryam, and Sohana mention these characteristics at the level of self-perception of the Kutchi Kohli community. It is important to mention that although they use the simple term of reference "Kutchi Kohli," they are including Christian and Hindu Kutchi Kohlis in it. This lack of distinction on the use of language is a clear sign of continuity and belonging.

## Exploring Indigenous Spirituality

Maryam mentions that "they are very helpful, honest, true people of God; they bring other people on the right path. Kutchi Kohli Christians visit the sick and pray with them and for them."[9] Sohana perceives that Kutchi Kohli Christians are "very strong in their spirituality and have strong faith in God." She also highlights that "Christians do not create any fear in the hearts of others; rather they give them the courage to have faith."

## Double Cultural and Religious Belonging

A second aspect that findings show is that Kutchi Kohli Christians are in a conscious double process. First, they are shaping their way of being Christian and second they try to do it without assuming another cultural identity. Thus, the data gathered during the interviews clearly show that Kutchi Kohli Christians are aware of who they are—Kutchi Kohlis. They are conscious of an ongoing process of changing religion,[10] but for them, this does not mean a radical change in their cultural, social identity, instead, they are trying to build bridges between these two belongings.

The participants consider that there are good things in the religion of their ancestors that they should not ignore. Thus, Prem stated, "This [Kutchi Kohli] is our culture and we are Kutchi, so we have to keep this. We need to always remember this, that we are Kutchi Kohli Christian, we are not Punjabi."[11] In the same vein, Mohan said,

> [Kutchi Kohli] Hindu traditions are very old. We can learn from them. The good things that are in them can be taken. We can take what is good and leave what is not.

---

9. The use of indirect language is a common characteristic of Kutchi Kohli and Urdu languages, even when referring to a reality in which the subject is involved or which the subject belongs to.

10. I am not referring to an ongoing process of conversion of Hindu Kutchi Kohlis to Christianity; what I am pointing out is that the identity formation process of the Kutchi Kohli Christian is an ongoing process.

11. The majority of Christians in Pakistan are Punjabis.

So the tradition of Hindu is not dangerous but that is good, and some things we can adapt.

Furthermore, he stated that "our Kutchi Kohli people easily accept what is good in other religions." These affirmations depict the tension always present in cases of multiple religious belonging concerning the acceptance or rejection of certain forms of heteronomy as constitutive of the new religious or cultural identity.[12]

The tension mentioned above is fully expressed when, for example, Maryam points out as negative that there are some Kutchi Kohlis who have become Christians, yet they continue practicing Hindu rites. She said, "Even in our colony[13] also there are some who do the rituals of Hinduism. And they make offerings in the names of Devs." In the same vein, Sonia thinks that "if they say they are Christians so they should remain Christians, rather than going back to Hinduism." However, she later nuances her opinion, stating that it is "fear present among Kutchi Kohli people, especially those who are weak in their Christian faith, and the fear created by the *bhopas* and *bhagats*[14] is the cause of this 'coming back' to Hindu practices."[15] For Sonia, "our hearts should be on Jesus and Mary; if we say we are Christians then there should not be any fear." These examples imply that for some of the participants, this double belonging involves the capacity to renounce certain socio-religious practices considered incompatible with the new religious identity. However, this capacity does not exclude tension

---

12. Cornille, "Double Religious Belonging," 39.

13. In the city of Tando Allahyar there is a property in which many Kutchi Kohli Christian families live; this land is named St. Joseph's Colony.

14. *Bhopas* are described as traditional healers. Cf. Banerjee et al., "Wealth, Health, and Health Services," 329. In Sindh, Pakistan, they also perform priestly and divination functions, and their healing powers are related to the divinities.

15. It is important to point out that this statement does not imply that all *bhopas* and *bhagats* are considered a source of tension in the daily life of Kutchi Kholi Christians or that they are enemies of Christianity. As a matter of fact, many of them collaborate with the Kutchi Kohli Christian community, and they can also be a helpful presence in the life of people.

Exploring Indigenous Spirituality

that can arise among the members of the Kutchi Kohli Christian community concerning this matter.

## Kutchi Kohli Christian Spirituality and Kutchi Kohli Spirituality

A third finding that is important to mention is how close the terms are in which the participants have described Kutchi Kohli spirituality and the spirituality of the Kutchi Kohli Christians. This proximity expresses the complexity and vitality of the relationship of Kutchi Kohli Christians with their *Kutchikohliness*. The following table aims to illustrate this closeness while respecting the differences.

| Interviewee | Kutchi Kohli Christian Spirituality | Kutchi Kohli Spirituality |
|---|---|---|
| Prem | The "Divine acting and present in us and in the world." "We see God in others." | "Entrust ourselves to God, complete trust in God." |
| Mohan | "Experience a compassionate God as a way to overcome fear." | "Fear of Dev and Devis." "The presence of spirits affecting life." |
| Sonia | "Reverence for Holy places, entering these places barefoot." | "Reverence for Holy places, entering these places barefoot." |
| Sohana | "We forgive and ask for forgiveness." "Love unites us." | "In the search for meaning," "pilgrimages," "believe in sharing, service, and in love." |
| Aakash | Spirituality "strongly related to the service of others." | "Devotional spirituality such as amulets and intercessions." |
| Maryam | Spiritual life "is marked by the experience of being redeemed." | "We value nature very much." |

## Ritual/Sacramental Dimension of Life

Another important area in which Kutchi Kohli Christians relate to their *Kutchikohliness* is the ritual/sacramental dimension of life.[16] The participants in the research pointed out two celebrations in which they related to their *Kutchikohliness* and which are important for their spiritual life and their identity as Kutchi Kohli Christians.

### *Joti Parab*[17]

All of the participants were aware of the Christian features of *Joti Parab* and of the importance of this celebration in the life of the Kutchi Kohli Christian community. They have mentioned that "*Joti Parab* celebrates the light of Christ which came to us to remove the darkness from our life." Four participants considered that "as Kutchi Kohli Hindus celebrate Diwali, so the concept of *Joti Parab* was created in order to finish[18] the gap of emptiness that those Kutchi Kohlis who are Christian could feel." It is important to notice that the link with the Hindu celebration of Diwali is not external but ontologically rooted in the interior experience of Kutchi Kohli Christians as the concept of inter-spirituality suggests.[19]

One important aspect that connects Diwali and *Joti Parab* is their reconciliatory character. Prem is aware of that and stated that Diwali "is a ritual of reconciliation among Hindus which we also celebrate[20] and it is about forgiveness and those who are angry with each other, for them to be reconciled." In the same vein, Mohan stated,

---

16. I use the term "sacramental" as a reference not to the seven sacraments of the Catholic Church but to the symbolic dimension of daily life. This symbolic dimension implies that common things, daily experiences, can lead us to the encounter with the divine as suggested by Boff in *Sacraments of Life*.

17. The word *joti* means "light" and *parab* means "feast." *Joti Parab* is the feast of the light.

18. They use the word "finish" instead of fill as a way to overcome the gap experienced by Kutchi Kohli Christians.

19. Teasdale, *Mystic Heart*, 27.

20. He is referring to *Joti Parab*.

## Exploring Indigenous Spirituality

> The purpose of Diwali in Hinduism is the reconciliation among those who are angry with each other; so in *Joti Parab* the same element of reconciliation has been taken. If people do not talk to each other in the family . . . so this element of reconciliation really helps a lot, and many people reconcile with each other; that is why we call it that the light of Christ has come into their lives. And that is *Joti Parab*.

It is important to underline the consciousness of the use of Hindu elements as a way of fostering their life socially and spiritually.

### *Wedding Rite*

The wedding rite is another example of how Kutchi Kohli Christians relate to their *Kutchikohliness*, but also how the phenomenon of multiple religious belonging is an appropriate category for understanding their internal dynamics. At the center of the discussion is the fact that *fera*[21] is performed during the Kutchi Kohli Christian weddings rites.[22] The participants are aware of the Hindu origin of this practice; thus Mohan mentions that

> the ritual of *fera* is very old and has come from Hinduism. Even my wedding was done like this. Our culture is like this, that without *fera* [a] wedding will look incomplete. We have made some additions in it, as Bible reading is done and vows are taken, so there is nothing Hindu in Christian *fera*.

It is interesting to notice in this statement the appropriation of Hindu elements as well as the recognition of belonging to a

---

21. *Fera* is the circular movement that the couples perform around the fire during the Hindu wedding rite. This circular movement gives legal validity to the marriage in some Hindu traditions.

22. The controversy is not principally among Kutchi Kohli Christians, even though some may not desire this practice. The controversy starts when Kutchi Kohli Christians have to interact with Punjabi Christians; many of them consider this practice as syncretic. So this section may be read not only in dialogue with Hindu Kutchi Kohlis, but also in dialogue with other Pakistani Christians.

larger community. In addition, Prem considers that *fera* is a cultural practice and not a Hindu one; he says, "*Fera* is just *fera* and there is nothing wrong in it. It is our culture as we are also Kutchi Kohlis, but in the *fera*, we have mingled the color of Christianity. So it is different than Hindu *fera*."

Other participants highlighted the difference introduced by Christianity in the wedding rite, pointing to the fact that *fera* is performed, but it has a new meaning now. Thus, Sonia stated,

> In Hindu *fera*, the couple just get the blessing of parents but they neither get blessings from a priest nor from Jesus, but in Christian *fera*, the blessing is from parents, priest, and Jesus and vows are taken and the priest prays whole-heartedly, which really brings blessings in the life of the couple.

Sohana highlights the same discontinuity with the Hindu practice.

## Building a Relationship with God: The Shaping of Interiority

The second area of systematization of the interviews is the way in which Kutchi Kohli Christians experience their relationship with God. This offers a glance into their interiority, into their spiritual lives.

### Personal Experience of God

The data show that as other indigenous people the Kutchi Kohlis use different terms to refer to God, either conceptually or spiritually.[23] The data also reveal an experience of closeness to God by those interviewed and a certain facility for establishing this relationship.

Names are not only ways in which the divine is denoted; they are first of all ways in which the divine is experienced. Thus, the

---

23. In their study of the Mayas, Ku Canche and his team identify that same dynamic. Cf. Ku Canche and Team, "Indigenous Theology," 194.

participants experience God predominantly as "father." Maryam said, "I call God my *Pita*.[24] God is everything for me and he is a very precious gift of my life." Prem describes his experience of God as the "Father [who] is presented in the story of the prodigal son; in that way, I call God as a *Reham kernar*[25] and *muaf kernar*[26] *Pita/Baap*."[27] This has cultural and social[28] connotations related to a patriarchal society, which are reaffirmed by Christian theology.

Mohan makes a more subtle distinction when he states, "I call God as *Bhagwan*,[29] then if I put *Isu Parbhu*[30] in front of me then he is my *Guru*.[31] But the place of God is higher so I know him as *Ishwar*,[32] *Baap*, and *Peda kernar*."[33] In the same vein, Sonia says,

> God for us is a *Peda kernar*, *Taranhar*,[34] Father who has given us life, this world and whatever we are, it is all because of him. He is our God and we are from him. There is no other who is ours.

Aakash mentioned that he uses different names for God. He said, "God for us is the *Peda kernar*, Creator of life and everything. He has created us in his own image. My life is from God. We understand God as a *Baap*. He is *Reham kernar*, he is *Zivato Bhagwan*,[35] and *Taranhar*. These are the names I call God with."

I left the Kutchi Kohli words in the main text in order not only to show the diversity but also the shared vocabulary among

24. Kutchi Kohli word for father.
25. Merciful.
26. Forgiving.
27. *Baap* is another word for father, as well as the Urdu word for father.
28. A common image among Kutchi Kohli people is to consider the father as a roof which provides shelter, support, and security to the individuals and to the group (family, clan, community).
29. One of the Kutchi Kohli words for God.
30. Terms use to refer to Jesus Christ.
31. Master and teacher.
32. Lord.
33. Creator.
34. Savior.
35. Living God.

Kutchi Kohlis. Furthermore, this diversity of names points to a rich and personal experience of the divine that should be considered in all its richness.

## Prayer Life/Role of Prayer in the Life of Kutchi Kohlis

Prayer plays a key role in the spiritual life of the participants, and they suggest the same role in the faith of Kutchi Kohli people. They show a strong belief in the power of prayer and they consider that God hears their prayers. However, the interviews also suggest that their prayers are not always heard immediately, but slowly, surely, they will be. Thus, for Prem prayer is an experience with God:

> I just talk to him the way I am talking to you. God does listen to my prayer when I pray for others and for myself. I feel his involvement in life, but it is not that all the prayers are heard, but those that are [heard] are for the good purpose of others and of myself.

Maryam and Sonia have a time set for their prayers. They consider that prayer is an important part of their life and that through prayer, growth takes place in their faith. Sonia says, "Because of our Christian faith, many changes have taken place in my family. We pray each morning and evening and light the incense in front of God. Our hearts become strong through prayer and we keep growing in our faith." A strong link between prayer and growth and healthy spiritual life is noticeable in the interviews.

Mohan and Sohana have a different approach to prayer. They think that during the day there can be different reasons where prayer is needed and they just say prayers on the spot. Sohana says, "Whenever my heart wants to remember God I just pray there and then. . . . If we do not pray for unnecessary things then surely God hears our prayer. He helps us with sickness and problems." In the same vein, Aakash describes the role of prayer in settling daily life issues. He states, "Many times we are surrounded by Satan and many problems come and sickness comes but through prayer, all get settled."

This depiction of their prayer life and the way the participants understand it offers an image of their interior journey and the ways in which they make sense of their life through their faith. Thus, their spiritual life is revealed as the locus of the humanization of their experiences (positives and negatives).

## Community and Family: A Ground for Spiritual Growth

The third area of systematization leads us to explore the ways in which the Catholic Church[36] and family environment help or block the spiritual life of Kutchi Kohli Christians. This is central for what Schneiders identifies as a key element of spirituality: a project of life. The environment will make it possible or not.

### Catholic Church as a Community Environment

The participants have experienced the Catholic Church as a community. For them, priests and sisters have played an important role in their lives and spiritual journeys, and they agree in mentioning that it is this community that makes Kutchi Kohli Christians strong in their Christian faith.[37]

Through the interviews, they have pointed out the importance of this bond created, first with priests and sisters and then with us as a community. Thus, Prem stated, "Fathers and sisters used to come to us and used to stay in our place. We became strong in our faith and spirituality by being with them." Similarly,

---

36. The Catholic Church in Sindh is organized in such a way that all the Kutchi Kohli Christians, although dispersed in a vast territory, are under the pastoral care of one group of priests, sisters, and catechists. This creates a sense of belonging to an identifiable community. The main geographical center for this community is the parish in Tando Allahyar, although there are other sub-units across the territory of the diocese of Hyderabad.

37. This role played by the Catholic Church can be found also among other indigenous peoples. Cf. Lopez Hernandez, "Teutlatolli: Speaking about God," 139–70.

Maryam said, "When I used to live in Akram colony[38] my father used to ask us to go to church and we all used to go as a family and fathers and sisters used to come to our house and used to pray; this helped us in the growth of our faith."

Sohana went further and said that the visits and faith-sharing of missionaries and masters were the reasons she became a Christian. She narrated,

> Before we used to live in Khipro, then another village. There, Father Brendan and Master Mansingh came. They came many times and I liked their religion and way of prayer, especially the Eucharist, and I felt the desire in my heart to become a Christian.

However, as mentioned above, this sense of community is not limited to the relationship with the priest and religious sisters. Thus, Mohan shared a difficult moment of his life and said, "My own Christian people came and saved me and brought me to my home."

This sense of belonging to a new community plays an important role in the spiritual life of the Kutchi Kohli Christian and provides them with a solid ground from which to interact with the larger Kutchi Kohli community as well as with Muslims and other Pakistani Christians.

## Spirituality and Family Environment

The data show the complexity of the family environment. All the participants have Hindu relatives, and, for example in the case of marriage, the belonging to the Kutchi Kohli community is considered primarily over the belonging to the Christian community.[39] Thus, on the one hand, a Christian family environment helps Kutchi Kohli Christians in their spiritual growth and in developing their faith. On the other hand, if they have to live with their Hindu

---

38. A sector of Tando Allahyar city where the parish for the Kutchi Kohlis was established.

39. Among Kutchi Kohlis, as well as among the majority of Pakistanis, marriages are arranged by the families and there is a complex set of rules that make one person suitable or not for marriage.

relatives or in-laws, as is the case for Maryam,[40] difficulties arise and their faith life becomes fragile.

This complexity of family relationships is depicted through the interviews. On a positive note, Mohan stated, "I have two girls and one son. And by seeing me, my daughters read the Bible, in fact, they read and pray more than I do . . . this faith has been transmitted to them." However, Sonia mentioned how difficult was for her to be a Christian at the beginning, but as her

> husband was a catechist, so [she] used to see him and sometimes [she] used to go with him to the *illaqa*[41] and pray. With him, [she] used to celebrate *Nataal parab* and *Pashka parab*;[42] this changed [her] and [she] grew in Christian faith.

For Maryam, life was more complex; she said,

> Before my marriage, my life was very good. I easily used to come to the church to pray, but I am married into a family who is pure Hindu, and in that village I was the only one Christian, and I went through so many problems, and many temptations came, but God looked after me.

Her experience shows the complexity and the ambiguity of relationships among Kutchi Kohli Hindus and Christians and of how this complexity affects their spiritual life. However, it is important to underline that this complexity is not lived in a passive manner; Kutchi Kohli Christians are agents of their own lives. In this vein, Liliana R. Goldin and Brent Metz in their study of Maya indigenous people mention that "this conversion is internal and personal; the 'acceptance' of a new belief system."[43]

---

40. I will consider her experience more in detail in another section in order to situate her experience in the larger context of the lives of Kutchi Kohli women.
41. Sector in which a parish is divided.
42. Christmas and Easter respectively.
43. Goldin and Metz, "Invisible Converts to Protestantism," 74.

## Interacting with People of Other Religions

The way in which the participants perceive their interaction with other religions, especially Hinduism and Islam, is the fourth area of systematization. In this section, two conceptual tools are preeminent for reading the interviews: double religious belonging and hybridization.

### A Complex Interaction with Hinduism

The data are quite rich in this area. First, it is important to mention that among the participants are both those who were born as Christians[44] and those who converted from Hinduism. This offers different angles to consider this interaction. Second, among Kutchi Kohlis, although there is a distinction between Christians and Hindus, being part of the ethnic group supersedes these other belongings. Thus, one interviewee stated, "For Kutchi Kohlis, [we] are Kutchi Kohli, before being Hindus or Christians." This makes common marriage between Christians and Hindus a social and religious interaction.

In this vein, Prem points out that "they[45] have to respect the rites of Kutchi Kohlis who are Hindus as they are also Kutchi Kohli." He adds, "Later on our children will be married in their families, so we have to be careful." He also highlights that for funerals or other ceremonies Christian and Hindu relatives gather together. However, he mentions that

> the whole night they pray. The priest usually goes [prays] first as at the time of the condolence ceremony when there is a mixed group of Christian and Hindu Kutchis;

---

44. I am conscious that this is a polemical statement. However, in the context of Pakistan, people are born not only in a country and in a family; we are born into an ethnic group and into a religious community. Although conversion is possible and legally allowed, the social consequences of this kind of decision are multiple and can even be a matter of life and death for the individuals. In addition, to be born Christian, Hindu, or Muslim is a constitutive element of the self.

45. Indirect use of pronouns in the Kutchi Kohli language.

the priest does not want to create problems among them, so they pray and read the Bible and sing hymns, then other *bhagats* come and pray. So we listen to their hymns also as they also have a good message and are similar to the Bible.

This example shows the dynamics of multiple religious belonging and inter-spirituality as lived by Kutchi Kohli Christians.

However, tensions are present in this interaction. Mohan mentioned that "with other relatives who are Hindus, we cannot talk to them about religion." Maryam goes further and states that Hindu religious authorities can manipulate Kutchi Kohli people.

> *Bhopas* create fear in the hearts of people and tell them that their dev and devis[46] are against Jesus, so do not send your children to the hostels because fathers are not good, and if your children get sick so it is because of them.

Aakash also underlines the tension experienced by Kutchi Kohli Christians, especially in their relationship with *bhagats*.[47] He said, "They try to pull us in their law of Hinduism, and they try that we do what they want, but we do not do that." Sohana also talked about the tension and the difference between a Catholic priest and a Hindu priest.[48] For her, "there is a tension between fathers and *bhagats* because when fathers go to someone's house to pray they do not take money but *bhagats* they do."

Taking these into consideration, it is possible to affirm that the interaction with Hinduism is not only complex, but it affects the self-understanding and the spiritual life of Kutchi Kohli Christians in both positive and negative ways.

---

46. Feminine and masculine divinities or spirits that form part of the Hindu pantheon of gods.

47. A *bhagat* is a Hindu religious man who performs rites such as funerals, prayers or reading of the *Bhagavad Gita*. He also sings religious songs called *bhajans*.

48. Bhagat.

## Living in the Land of the Pure: Pakistan as Islamic

The interaction with Islam occurs at multiple layers, including the fact of living in an Islamic country,[49] the constant interaction with Muslims, and the cultural background of Sindh with its particular kind of Islam.[50]

Concerning the daily interaction with Muslims, the participants pointed out a positive general appreciation of them, but also the need to be cautious. Thus, Prem mentioned that his

> experience with Muslims is very good and I believe that they are very good people. As we are not powerful so they keep our people for a job as they think that we are honest. In the past, Muslims did not used to like us and they used to hate us, but now it has changed.

Maryam thinks that "some Muslims are good and some are bad. Because of some Muslims, we suffer and some are against Jesus." Mohan said, "They are the ones who protect us during our festivals. . . . They accept or not, but they know in their heart that we are good and peaceful people." Sonia highlights their faith: "Muslims are strong in their faith and we are strong in our faith, so we do not worry about them." For Aakash, "it is not difficult to live with Muslims, but we need to be careful."

The participants express deep respect for Islamic practices. Prem said, "I have gone to Sehwan, Bhit Shah, and Oderelal[51] and I understand that these people are meant to be respected."

It is noticeable that the way in which they perceive their relationship with Muslims is less ambiguous and tense than their relationship with Hindus. Furthermore, for the participants, the ways in which the Islamic setting of Pakistan shapes their lives,

---

49. This is from the legal point of view that established that Pakistan is an Islamic state.

50. Islam in Sindh has a strong Sufi character. In addition, there has been much interaction between Islamic tenets and cultural elements of peoples who inhabited this province of Pakistan.

51. These three places are Sufi shrines visited by Christians, Hindus, and Muslims through the year and form part of the spiritual life of people in Sindh.

practices, the vision of the world, and spiritual experience are less evident. What can be noticed as part of a process of hybridization by researchers is not evident for the Kutchi Kohli Christians participating in this research.

## Challenges and Obstacles for Spiritual Growth and Life

Finally, it is important to mention some challenges and/or obstacles for the spiritual life of the Kutchi Kohli Christians that can be deduced from the data.

### The Complex Role of *Bhopas* and *Bhagats*

The data gathered from the interviews clearly present the role of *bhopas* and *bhagats* as an obstacle for the growth of Kutchi Kohli people, whether they are Hindus or Christians. Five of the six participants have clearly mentioned that *bhopas* and *bhagats* are an obstacle for their spiritual growth and that the tool that they use is fear. Thus, Prem stated, "The first obstacle [for his spiritual life] are *bhopas*." Maryam said, "*Bhagats* and *bhopas* do not let them grow in Christian spirituality."

For Mohan, "those who do all these rituals,[52] they are made afraid; if you will not do this, then this will happen. *Bhopas* create this fear in their hearts." Sonia agrees and says, "The fear which is created by *bhopas* does not allow them to be strong in their faith, because they believe in them and become afraid that if they will not do something, so *bhopa* will punish them and do magic on them; for that reason their hearts are afraid." Sohana goes further and considers that *bhopas* and *bhagats* "are both after the Christian faith. They stop people from coming into Christianity."

It is interesting to point out that in the context of Maya indigenous people, their "healers" or "witch-doctors," sometimes called "the wise priests," also try to prevent people from leaving

---

52. Christian or Hindu Kutchi Kohlis.

the religion of their ancestors.⁵³ Are *bhopas* and *bhagats* a case of cultural resistance or a defense of structures of oppression?⁵⁴

## Sickness and Spirituality

The Kutchi Kohli understanding of sickness is different from the Western one, and it is changing. Kutchi Kohli people used to think that sickness was a kind of punishment they received when they did something wrong. However, the data show that among Kutchi Kohli Christians, sickness is taken as sickness and they go to the doctors. Nevertheless, they strongly believe that in sickness, prayer is important. Thus, Sonia and Maryam agree that "when sickness comes on them, so they do not go to the *bhopas* but they go to the doctors, and if they do not get well they come to the priests."

Aakash commented, "90% Christians do not go to *bhopa* if sickness comes, they go to the doctor and come to the priest to pray. But Hindus think that if they will go to *bhopa* then they will be well."

Sickness is a moment of fragility that can be a major upsetting experience for those belonging to vulnerable cultures. For this reason not only a supernatural explanation is plausible for them, but also fear facing these moments of fragility makes people look for all available options for healing.⁵⁵ This represents a real and constant challenge for the spiritual life of Kutchi Kohli Christians.

## Spirituality and Oppression

The data show the awareness of the participants about the way structures of oppression affect their lives at all levels.

---

53. Garcia Ruiz, "Ethnic Resistance and the Maya Calendar," 94.
54. This area may need further study.
55. A similar understanding of sickness is pointed out among people of Chiapas in Ortega, "'A Nation Where Everyone Has a Place,'" 278.

Exploring Indigenous Spirituality

*Social Structure as an Obstacle for Spiritual Life*

Prem mentioned the injustice the landlords[56] do to Kutchi Kohli people as they are not paid properly: "The landlords do not give to people what they have earned. From 100 rupee they just give 25 rupees and keep 75 to themselves; that is why Kutchi people are poor." Furthermore, Mohan affirms that "if we are working under them, then we have to accept all and even if we do not want to do still we have to say yes." Sonia points out clearly the injustice done to the Kutchi Kohlis:

> They are very poor and are in the debt of the landlord. The whole family work under the landlord but still they do not get enough, and many times they sleep hungry because they are not paid what is their right. The farmers tell the landlord to give them money but still, they are not given, then they just keep quiet and bear all the injustice. They live a very painful life. They work under the landlord but they ask others [for money] to survive.

Furthermore, she feels that more prayers are needed to give them strength, but besides that, they have to be brave to fight for their rights:

> They need to become strong. They consider themselves weak so that is why they do not raise their voices against the unjust system. They need to trust God and pray more and help themselves for their rights.

This is a central point for understanding Kutchi Kohli Christian spirituality. The "internalized oppression"[57] and its dehumanizing consequences undermine the agency of the Kutchi Kohlis and block their capacity for entering into a dynamic of authenticity as

---

56. Pakistan, and especially the province of Sindh, has a feudal social structure in which a few families are owners of vast tracts of land, and people, like the Kutchi Kohlis who work for them, live on their lands. In Sindh these landlords are also linked to the religious shrines that shape the spiritual landscape of the province.

57. O'Brien, *Hope That Is Still with Us*, 115.

described by Michael O'Sullivan.[58] The participants are conscious of this problem, and that can be the starting point for a healing journey.

## Spirituality and Women

The participants related the theme of oppression with the situation of Kutchi Kohli women. Four participants highlighted the following areas of oppression.

1. Their oppressed condition.

Maryam, who was married into a Hindu family, has been tortured a lot, but she did not let go of her own Christian faith and her trust in Jesus. She stated,

> My in-laws tortured me very much and asked me to pray to Hindu gods and said that because of your faith in Jesus your children are dying so leave Jesus, but I never left Jesus. I also fell sick and many problems came in my life, and my in-laws brought the thread[59] from the *bhopa* and asked me to tie that to myself but I refused to do that. They said to me that my Jesus has made me mad and asked me to leave our house. They told me to break the relation with them if I wanted to keep the relationship with Jesus. "Do not stay at our house." I said to them that I will leave all of you but I will not leave Jesus.

From her sharing, it is obvious how difficult it can be for a Christian girl to be married into a Hindu family. Maryam also mentioned her sister, who was in the same situation and could not fight for her faith: "She left Jesus because of the difficulties came in her life."

This painful reality is not exclusive to Kutchi Kohli women; other indigenous women go through similar or worse situations. In the research done on the Maya women, Dalila C. Nayap-Pot points out that "social oppression is somehow related to the oppression

---

58. O'Sullivan, "'Authenticity,'" 6.
59. Used as an amulet against bad spirits, sickness, and misfortunes.

of women."[60] Furthermore, she also mentions that "indigenous women have been known for their silence [more] than for their outward resistance."[61] These are important points to consider in the journey to empower Kutchi Kohlis.

2. The role of Jesus in women's lives.

Sonia underlines the impact of Jesus' relationship with women in her life. She feels that Jesus cares for their dignity, women as women. She says, "Women feel proud that Jesus gave importance and love to women, while in Hinduism Krishna and even *bhopas* see women with wrong eyes [lust]." A similar finding is presented by Dalila C. Nayap-Pot, who recounts that many Maya women became Christian because they found the life of Jesus identifying with their social context: "They sense that He accompanies them in their daily lives."[62]

3. The change regarding the age of marriage of women.

Aakash pointed out that a change has taken place in the Kutchi Kohli people regarding the marriage age of girls. They were married at a very early age before, but now "we have made the rule not to marry the girl before 18 years."[63]

4. The role of education in empowering Kutchi Kohli women.

Prem pointed out the role of education in the development of Kutchi Kohli girls and how it made people value education. He stated that "sisters [nuns] have helped in the education of girls. In the beginning, the parents did not allow their daughters to go out of their houses but now they trust us [Christians] and send their daughters to us for education in the hostel."

As with other problems faced by Kutchi Kohli women, they are not the only ones suffering these difficulties in the world. Dalila

60. Nayap-Pot, "Social Role of Maya Women," 103.

61. Nayap-Pot, "Social Role of Maya Women," 104.

62. Nayap-Pot, "Social Role of Maya Women," 110.

63. In many areas of Pakistan (Sindh, Baluchistan, KPK) the practice is marrying girls under sixteen years old. So this change is a considerable social and cultural effort to move in a new direction.

C. Nayap-Pot has pointed out that Maya women "live in rural areas where illiteracy, ignorance of their rights, and the weight of home and family tasks and responsibilities add to their burdens."[64]

---

64. Nayap-Pot, "Social Role of Maya Women," 104.

# 4

# Paths towards the Future

THE AIM OF THIS research is to highlight the main aspects of Kutchi Kohli Christian spirituality and identify ways to empower their spiritual, communitarian, and social growth. The participants were Catholic Christians belonging to an indigenous group living in Sindh province, in southern Pakistan: the Kutchi Kohlis. The findings show a complex and rich interior life that is shaped in a personal journey of light and shadows, hopes and distress. In this journey, Kutchi Kohli Christians have to also engage with other religions and with an unjust social structure that affects them as well as shapes their spiritual life.

## Expected and Unexpected Results

The interviews have confirmed some of the research hypotheses and expectations. Firstly, the research confirms that Kutchi Kohli Christians are in the process of building up their Christian identity in interaction with their *Kutchikohliness*. In order to achieve this, they have to establish a constant dialogue with their being Christian, with their Hindu relatives, with their ethnic identity, and, finally, with their Pakistani citizenship. Thus, the participants are aware that they are making choices (at the ritual, social, and spiritual levels) that will determine who they are as Christians, as

Kutchi Kohlis, and as Pakistanis. On this level it is also important to notice the role education plays in the forming of this identity; all the participants have pointed out that access to education has been the key for creating the conditions of possibility for building this new identity in interaction with their *Kutchikohliness*.

Secondly, the interviews have confirmed that the relationship with the Hindu Kutchi Kohlis is ongoing and complex. On the positive side, there is a shared feeling of belonging to one community: the Kutchi Kohlis. This allows intermarriage, sharing joys and sorrows, and living and working together. In addition, this sense of belonging allows Kutchi Kohli Christians to incorporate elements and symbols coming from Kutchi Kohli Hindu spiritual, devotional, and ritual life into their Christian spiritual and ritual life. Thus, it is possible to state at this level that Kutchi Kohli Christians' spiritual experience is shaped by a creative articulation of three sources: (i) the Christian faith received mostly from foreign missionaries, (ii) the Hindu environment of family, village, or social setting, and (iii) the cultural elements coming from Kutchi Kohli culture. I think this creative articulation is neither a form of syncretism nor the outcome of an inculturation strategy, but rather it is grounded on the existential experience that in these three sources there are life-giving elements that nourish the spiritual life of Kutchi Kohli Christians. On the challenging side, this relationship is problematic and can even create conflict among family members, leading to painful situations. In addition, this sense of belonging to the Kutchi Kohli community goes hand in hand with a sense of belonging to a new community—the community of Kutchi Kohli Christians. This double belonging, although it can produce tension, is the ground for personal and communitarian growth.

Thirdly, the research has pointed out *fear* as one of the main obstacles hindering the spiritual growth of Kutchi Kohli Christians and the relationship between Christian and Hindu Kutchi Kohlis. It is important to point out that fear is related to two main sources: (i) sickness and (ii) the actions of some Hindu religious leaders (*bhopas* and *bhagats*). Fear related to sickness underlines the very real fragility of life among Kutchi Kohlis who, lacking access to appropriate health services, experience sickness as leading many to death. As a consequence of this, their spiritual journey is not only blocked, but they are also weak under the religious pressure of *bhopas* and *bhagats*, who interpret their sickness as the result of their being Christian. Thus, the vulnerability experienced by Kutchi Kohli Christians is not only physical but also spiritual. Consequently, any proposal for empowering them needs to take this reality seriously.

Fourthly, the interviews have confirmed that there is an internalized oppression that affects the spiritual life of Kutchi Kohli Christians. The causes of internalized oppression differ between men and women; for men it is experienced mostly through the social structure (at work, in the relationship with the landlords, and so forth), whereas for women it is at their workplaces but also within families, especially when a Kutchi Kohli Christian girl is married into a Hindu family, as we can see in the narrative of Maryam. Another aspect of internalized oppression affecting especially women is the fact that Pakistani cultures are structurally patriarchal; this characteristic is strengthened by the ways in which Christianity, Hinduism, and Islam are structured and organized in Pakistan.

Finally, the participants have shared about their deep relationship with God and their prayer life without using the words "interiority" or "spirituality." However, the interviews clearly suggest that alongside the exteriority of religious practices, they have a deep interiority which is a source of strength and wisdom for facing the challenges and problems of life. It is this dimension that needs to be cultivated as a way of empowerment.

In addition to this, the research has provided some unexpected results. First, the tension between Kutchi Kohli Christians and Kutchi Kohli Hindus was highlighted more than any tension with Muslims. In a context in which religious minorities (Christians, Hindus, Sikhs, etc.) are used in the media and in the political sphere to illustrate the oppression of the Islamic context in Pakistan, the interviews reveal that at the spiritual level Christian

Kutchi Kohlis experience their relationship with Hindu Kutchi Kohlis as fragile and sometimes problematic.

Second, although the aim of the research is to explore Kutchi Kohli Christians' spirituality, the inner depth the participants demonstrated at the moment of sharing their own spiritual experiences was unexpected. They were able to use metaphors in order to convey their experience properly and clearly. They recognized processes and changes across time and generations; as their spirituality is evolving with the passage of time, they are conscious that some of its characteristics differ from the experiences of their elders. Furthermore, they were able to have a self-critical approach to their spiritual experiences in order to find ways to grow in their spiritual life.

## Emerging Themes and Existing Literature

The findings are linked with the literature review in many ways. Themes such as religious identity and cultural identity, interiority, belonging, interaction with the religious other, and oppression have been pointed out by the participants to a greater or lesser extent. Catherine Cornille has pointed out the importance of exploring the way in which multiple belongings are articulated by individuals and groups, as well as how this articulation shapes the identity and the spiritual life of people.[1]

Baruch Shimoni, in analyzing the processes of hybridization, has highlighted how cultures are changing continuously through interactions, negotiations, and mutual enrichment.[2] This process is clearly identifiable among Kutchi Kohli Christians.

The element of oppression has been treated by John O'Brien in his study of Punjabi Christians, underlining how this affects the spiritual and social life of Christians.[3] This reality is also present in the life of Kutchi Kohli Christians.

1. Cf. p. 12.
2. Cf. p. 14.
3. Cf. p. 6.

## Exploring Indigenous Spirituality

The shaping of one's own personal and/or collective identity is a central process in an emerging/young community. In this process, Claude Geffré suggests a double direction process in which both actors are enriched and transformed. He quotes Cardinal Malula, Archbishop of Kinshasa, who used to talk about the importance of Africanizing Christianity in contrast to Christianizing Africa.[4] In the same vein, I think Kutchi Kohli Christians are in the processes of appropriating Christianity, making and shaping Kutchi Kohli Christianity (*Kutchikohlinized* Christianity).

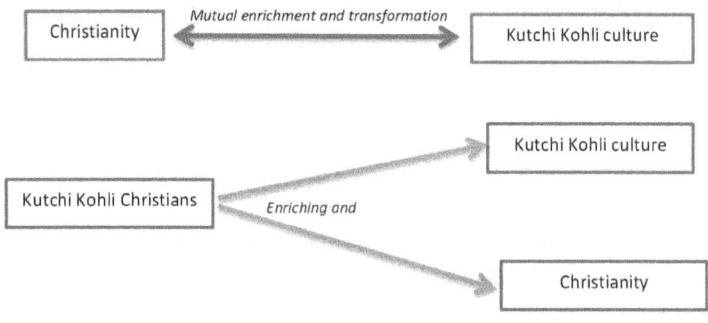

**Identity Processes among Kutchi Kohli Christians**

## Strengths and Limitations

Now I would like to highlight some of the strengths and limitations of the research process. Firstly, I myself being a Kutchi Kohli Christian has facilitated the interviews, allowing the participants to feel comfortable, speak freely, and go deeper in their sharing. Speaking in the Kutchi Kohli language and in Urdu also has allowed the participants to use their vocabulary and images for describing their spiritual life. In addition, the atmosphere of mutual trust in the interviews has made it possible for the participant not only to talk about their spiritual experiences but also to have

---

4. Cf. p. 13.

a critical approach to them. This has enriched the research and opens new horizons for further work.

Secondly, the desire and availability of the participants to talk and share their experiences of their spiritual journey have played an important role in this research. It was the first time that someone interviewed them or even invited them to talk about their spiritual lives. It has also been helpful that this was the first academic research conducted on their spirituality; thus, they were willing to explore this dimension of their lives.

Thirdly, at the methodological level, the open-ended/semi-structured interview allowed the participants to narrate freely their spiritual journey. Considering the structural and conceptual differences between English and the Kutchi Kohli language, another kind of interview may have reduced the possibilities to explore Kutchi Kohli Christian spirituality.

Fourthly, it was difficult to share with participants the conceptual framework of the research, this being due to the lack of appropriate terminology in Urdu and Kutchi Kohli.

Finally, sometimes it was difficult for the participants to articulate or formulate their relationship with Islam. They seemed unaware of how much the Islamic environment shaped their spiritual life.

## Further Research

Considering the originality of this research on the Kutchi Kohli Christians and in general regarding the Kutchi Kohlis of Pakistan, this work has opened new areas for further research. I would like to point out some of these areas that need further research.

- The spirituality of Kutchi Kohlis belonging to many Christian denominations. This will provide a deeper understanding of Kutchi Kohli Christian spirituality.

- The contemporary spirituality of Hindu Kutchi Kohlis, their impact on Kutchi Kohli Christians, and how the interaction of these two communities of Kutchi Kohlis shape each other.

- The manner in which Kutchi Kohli Christian spirituality is evolving across generations. In addition to this, it would be interesting to consider the impact of urbanization and of education upon Kutchi Kohli Christian spirituality.
- Kutchi Kohli women's spirituality and their role in the processes of bringing change in the Kutchi Kohli socio-cultural structure and in spiritual growth among Kutchi Kohlis.
- The manner in which the current cultural and socioeconomic transformations in Pakistan affect and transform what we have denominated *Kutchikohliness*.
- Finally, it would be important to study the similarities, differences, and articulations among the spiritual journeys of Kutchi Kohlis, Parkari Kohlis, Marwari, and Sindhi Bhils living in Pakistan.

## Recommendations

As mentioned previously, the present research also aims to identify ways to empower Kutchi Kohli Christians. In this vein, I would like to present some recommendations.

First, there is a great need for psychological and spiritual healing among Christian Kutchi Kohlis, as well as among Hindu Kutchi Kohlis. However, the cultural block for sharing about personal matters makes this endeavor quite a challenge. Thus, I think it is necessary to make spiritual accompaniment and counseling available to them. The confidential space created through this could allow them to narrate their lives, including their woundedness. Furthermore, these kinds of healing relationships can contribute to a deeper awareness of the internalized oppression experienced by Kutchi Kohlis.

Second, I think that it is important to walk with Kutchi Kohli Christians in their journey of building a deep interior life. In order to achieve this, it would be necessary to go beyond religious instruction and move towards spiritual formation; unfortunately, this dimension is not currently developed, and even for many Kutchi Kohli Christians, the word "spirituality" is unknown. Furthermore, any spiritual formation among Kutchi Kohlis may be a spirituality that empowers them in a context of poverty and social oppression.

Third, to empower the Kutchi Kohli Christian community requires cultivating the feminine dimension of spirituality. I do not refer only to empowering women, but to a reappraisal of what femininity actually is among Kutchi Kohlis. In order to achieve this, it would be necessary to go back to the multiple sources of Kutchi Kohli Christians: their Christian tradition, their *Kutchikohliness*, and the Hindu substratum of their spiritual experience.

Fourth, empowerment would not be possible without healing the self-perception and ethnic identity of Kutchi Kohli Christians. It would be important to create spaces that allow them to understand themselves, to know their culture in order to overcome the shame created by multiple oppressions and prejudices. This could lead them to discover the beauty and goodness of their *Kutchikohliness*.

Fifth, the findings have highlighted the complexity of the relationship between Christian and Hindu Kutchi Kohlis. There is a shared feeling of being part of one group; however, sometimes there is also a tense relationship. Following Schneiders's definition of spirituality, I think that it is possible to appeal to this shared human dimension, which has been shaped by a common cultural substratum. This could lead to building among Kutchi Kohlis a spirituality of reconciliation that respects the difference of each one and allows Kutchi Kohlis not only to live together but to grow together.

Finally, I would like to mention that this research has been one of the few spaces in which Kutchi Kohli Christians have been allowed to narrate and share their spiritual life. I think the creation of spaces is important, for instance, creating workshops that would allow Kutchi Kohli Christians to share their spiritual experiences. Furthermore, I think there is need to build capacities among Kutchi Kohli Christians at the level of spiritual formation and care in order to make it possible for them to assume the responsibility of caring for their own spiritual journey.

## Conclusion

The aim of this research was to study contemporary Kutchi Kohli Christian spirituality through an in-depth, detailed, qualitative study of a small group of individuals with a view to providing resources for the community's empowerment.

At the conceptual level, the research has shown the suitability of approaching the Kutchi Kohlis from the perspective of indigenous spirituality. This does not only offer an appropriate understanding of who the Kutchi Kohlis are as a people, but it can also contribute to a more healthy and fruitful self-understanding among Kutchi Kohlis. Furthermore, the conceptual and spiritual framework used in this research has revealed itself as being adequate for:

i. understanding the way in which Kutchi Kohli Christian identity and spiritual life are shaped as a result of complex and dynamic interactions with other communities and religious traditions.

ii. apprehending spirituality not as a religiously bound dimension, but as a dimension of the human condition that opens individuals to a broader horizon and project perspective (cf. Sandra Schneiders). In addition, this approach can contribute towards a foundational building of harmonious relations among Kutchi Kohlis, both Christian and Hindu.

At the epistemological level, the research reveals the importance of considering *Kutchikohliness* as a dynamic and constitutive element of Kutchi Kohli Christian spiritual life. However, it is important to underline that this term does not refer to an essential and static set of attributes, but refers to a reality in constant transformation, as has been described above.

At the methodological level, a narrative research approach has made it possible to identify the main elements of Kutchi Kohli

Christian spirituality. In particular, this approach has allowed the participants to express their views and experiences using their own terminology. I consider this to be essential for the study of the spirituality of an indigenous people, especially those who have mostly developed their sense of self (collective and individual) relying on an oral culture.

At the level of applied spirituality, the research has identified areas that can be developed in order to contribute to the empowerment of Kutchi Kohli Christians at the spiritual and social levels.

Finally, I would like to point out that this research constitutes the first study of Kutchi Kohli Christian spirituality and in general of Kutchi Kohli spirituality as a specific field of study. In the perspective of spirituality as a whole-life project, the study of Kutchi Kohli Christian spirituality can be a contribution to the study of indigenous spiritualities, but also to the life of Kutchi Kohli Christians in their endeavor of building a project of life integration and self-transcendence for them and for the Kutchi Kohli community.

# Appendix 1

## Questionnaire in English

1. Exploring Personal Experiences.
    a. History of faith
        i. I would like to know about your life as a Christian.
        ii. About your family: are they Christian too? When did they become Christian?
    b. Spiritual experience
        iii. It is always difficult to speak about our experience of God, but how would you describe your relationship with God?
        iv. Which images would you use to describe God? Who is God for you?
        v. Can you tell me about your prayer? How do you pray? When? Does your prayer touch/affect your daily life?
    c. Interactions with other faiths
        vi. How would you describe the faith of your parents, grandparents? Their hopes, their relationship with God? [Reference to the faith of their Hindu ancestors]

vii. What do the celebration of the light (Diwali—Christian equivalent), or the rites during the wedding ceremony mean for you at the spiritual level?

viii. Have you ever visited the shrine of Odero Lal [or other shrines around the Kutchi Kohli region]? How would you describe your experience there? How do you think your visits enhance the spiritual life of people?

2. Exploring general perceptions about the spiritual life of Kutchi Kohlis

    a. How will you describe the spiritual life of Kutchi Kohlis in general and specifically that of Kutchi Kohli Christians?
    b. What do you think are the main characteristics of the spiritual life of the Kutchi Kohli Christians?
    c. What do you think are the main differences (in relation with their spiritual life) between the first Kutchi Kohli Christians and the new generation?
    d. What do you think about the spiritual practices (devotions) of the Kutchi Kohli Christians?
    e. How do you think the spiritual life of the Kutchi Kohli Christians can be enhanced/fostered?
    f. What do you think about the Hindu traditions of the Kutchi Kohli people? Can these enhance the spiritual life of the Kutchi Kohli Christians?
    g. What do you think are the main challenges and obstacles for fostering the spiritual life of the Kutchi Kohli Christians?
    h. How would you describe the spiritual experience of people who visit the *dargah* of Rama Pir?
    i. What do you think are the most important and enriching elements of the Kutchi Kohli culture for the spiritual life of the Kutchi Kohli Christians?
    j. What do you think are the positive and negative contributions of Muslims' spiritual life in Sindh to the spiritual life of the Kutchi Kohli Christians?

# Appendix 2

## Data Analysis Procedure and Thematic Results

As indicated in the methodological framework, I analyzed the data of the interviews using NVivo data analysis software. The following is a description of the procedure.

# Appendix 2

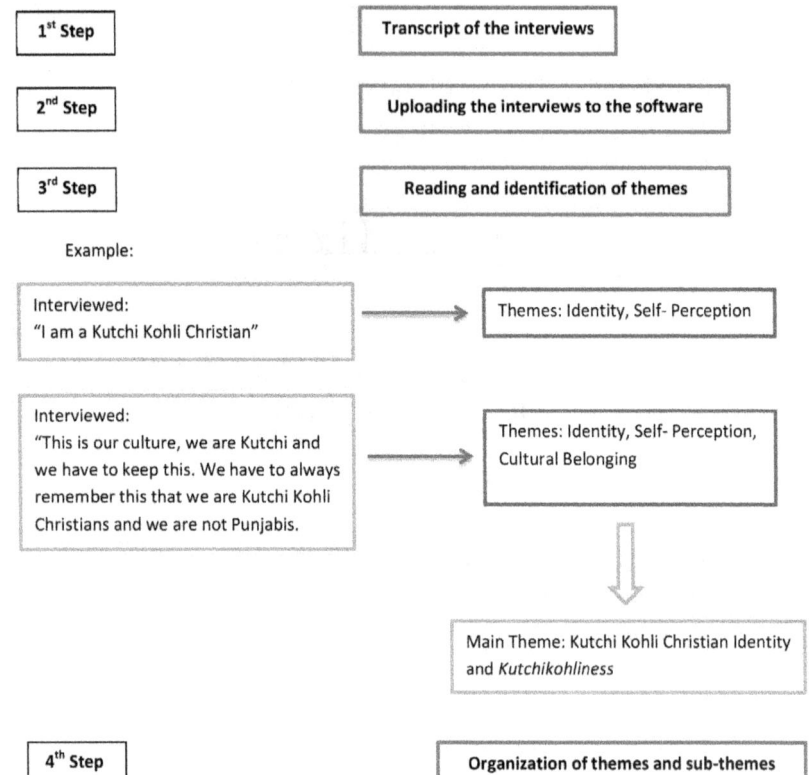

*Data Analysis Procedure and Thematic Results*

Thematic results of the analysis:

| | Main Theme | 2nd Thematic Level | 3rd Thematic Level |
|---|---|---|---|
| 1 | Kutchi Kohli Christian identity and *Kutchikohliness* | Identity and Self-Perception | |
| | | Double Cultural and Religious Belonging | |
| | | Kutchi Kohli Christian Spirituality and Kutchi Kohli Spirituality | |
| | | Ritual/Sacramental Dimension of Life | *Joti Parab* |
| | | | Wedding Rite |
| 2 | Building a Relationship with God: The Shaping of Interiority | Personal Experience of God | |
| | | Prayer Life, Role of Prayer in the Life of Kutchi Kohlis | |
| 3 | Community and Family a Ground for Spiritual Growth | Catholic Church as a Community Environment | Shaping of a New Collective Identity |
| | | Spirituality and Family Environment | Positive Perspectives and Experiences |
| | | | Positive Perspectives and Experiences |

# Appendix 2

| | Main Theme | 2nd Thematic Level | 3rd Thematic Level |
|---|---|---|---|
| 4 | Interacting with the Religious Others | A Complex Interaction with Hinduism | Positive Perspectives and Experiences |
| | | | Negative Perspectives and Experiences |
| | | Living in the Land of the Pure: Pakistan as an Islamic Country | Positive Appreciation |
| | | | Difficulty for Articulating This Relationship |
| 5 | Challenges and Obstacles for Spiritual Growth and Life | Role of *Bhopas* and *Bhagats* | Role of Fear |
| | | Sickness and Spirituality | Fragility of Life |
| | | Spirituality and Oppression | Social Structure as an Obstacle for Spiritual Life |
| | | | Spirituality and Women |

# Appendix 3

## Photos of Kutchi Kohlis

Kutchi Kohli Woman Preparing Food. © Emmanuel Guddu

## Appendix 3

Kutchi Kohli Christian Wedding. ©Emmanuel Guddu

Kutchi Kohli Christian Wedding. ©Emmnauel Guddu

## Photos of Kutchi Kohlis

Kutchi Kohli Christian Couple Performing *Fera*. © Emmanuel Guddu

# Glossary

| | |
|---|---|
| *Assalam-o Alaikum* | Greetings among Muslims (lit. "Peace be with you"). |
| *Baap* | Father. |
| *Bhagat* | Hindu religious man, who performs rites such as funerals, prayers, or reading of the *Bhagavad Gita* and who also sings the religious songs. |
| *Bhagwan* | God. |
| *Bhajans* | Religious songs. |
| *Bhopas* | Hindu healers. |
| *Biradheri* | Community, brotherhood, nation, or people. Commonly used to refer to a group of people united by blood, caste, or religion in Pakistan. |
| *Dargha* | Shrine of a Sufi saint. |
| *Dev* | god. |
| *Devi* | goddess. |
| *Fera* | Circular movement around fire a performed by a couple during a wedding. |
| *Guru* | Master/Teacher. |
| *Ishwar* | Lord. |

## Glossary

| | |
|---|---|
| *Illaqa* | A sector in which a parish is divided. |
| *Isu Ni Jai* | Greeting among the Kutchi Kohli Christians (lit. "Praise to Jesus"). |
| *Isu Parbhu* | Jesus Christ. |
| *Joti* | Light. |
| *Muaf Kernar* | Forgiving. |
| *Nataal Parab* | Christmas. |
| *Parab* | Feast. |
| *Pashka Parab* | Easter. |
| *Peda Kernar* | Creator. |
| *Pita* | Father. |
| *Reham Kernar* | Merciful. |
| *Taranhar* | Savior. |
| *Zivto Bhagwan* | Living God. |

# Bibliography

Ariarajah, S. Wesley. "Hindu Spirituality: An Invitation to Dialogue?" *The Ecumenical Review* 38.1 (2010) 75–81. https://doi.org/10.1111/j.1758-6623.1986.tb03401.x.

Bahr, Ann Marie. *Indigenous Religions*. Illustrated ed. Philadelphia: Chelsea House, 2004.

Banerjee, Abhijit, et al. "Wealth, Health, and Health Services in Rural Rajasthan." *American Economic Review* 94.2 (2004) 326–30. https://doi.org/10.1257/0002828041301902.

Barth, Fredrick. *Ethnic Groups and Boundaries*. Boston: Little, Brown and Company, 1969.

Bazeley, Pat, and Kristi Jackson. *Qualitative Data Analysis with NVivo*. 2nd ed. London: SAGE, 2013.

Behar-Horenstein, Linda S., and Ronald R. Morgan. "Narrative Research, Teaching, and Teacher Thinking: Perspectives and Possibilities." *Peabody Journal of Education* 70.2 (1995) 139–61. https://www.jstor.org/stable/1492852.

Boff, Leonardo. *Sacraments of Life, Life of the Sacraments: Story Theology*. Translated by J. Drury. Washington, DC: Pastoral, 1988.

Bradford, Collette. "Towards an Interspirituality Solution in a Healthcare Setting: Snapshots on a Journey." Master's thesis, Milltown Institute of Theology and Philosophy, 2009.

Clandinin, D. Jean, and M. Shaun Murphy. "Relational Ontological Commitments in Narrative Research." *Educational Researcher* 38.8 (2009) 598–602. https://www.jstor.org/stable/25592174.

Cook, Garrett, and Thomas Offit. "Pluralism and Transculturation in Indigenous Maya Religion." *Ethnology* 47.1 (2008) 45–59. https://www.jstor.org/stable/25651545.

Cornille, Catherine. "Double Religious Belonging: Aspects and Questions." *Buddhist-Christian Studies* 23 (2003) 43–49. https://www.jstor.org/stable/1390362.

———, ed. *Many Mansions? Multiple Religious Belonging and Christian Identity*. Eugene, OR: Wipf and Stock, 2010.

# Bibliography

Coulter, Cathy A. "Finding the Narrative in Narrative Research." *Educational Researcher* 38.8 (2009) 608–11. https://www.jstor.org/stable/25592176.

"COVID-19 and Indigenous Peoples." United Nations, March 30, 2020. https://www.un.org/development/desa/indigenouspeoples/covid-19.html.

Coward, Harold. "Hindu Spirituality and the Environment." *Journal for the Study of Religion, Nature and Culture—Ecotheology* 3 (1997) 50–60. https://doi.org/10.1558/ecotheology.v2i1.50.

Cox, James L. *From Primitive to Indigenous: The Academic Study of Indigenous Religions*. New York: Routledge, 2017.

Flanagan, Bernadette, and Michael O'Sullivan. "Spirituality in Contemporary Ireland: Manifesting Indigeneity." *Spiritus: A Journal of Christian Spirituality* 16.2A (2016) 55–73. https://doi.org/10.1353/scs.2016.0051.

Frohlich, Mary. "Spiritual Discipline, Discipline of Spirituality: Revisiting Questions of Definition and Method." In *Minding the Spirit: The Study of Christian Spirituality*, edited by Elizabeth A. Dreyer and Mark S. Burrows, 65–78. Baltimore: Johns Hopkins University Press, 2005.

Garcia Ruiz, Jesus. "Ethnic Resistance and the Maya Calendar." In *Crosscurrents in Indigenous Spirituality: Interface of Maya, Catholic and Protestant Worldviews*, edited by Guillermo Cook, 91–100. Leiden: Brill, 1997.

Geffré, Claude. "Double Belonging and the Originality of Christianity as a Religion." In *Many Mansions? Multiple Religious Belonging and Christian Identity*, edited by Catherine Cornille, 93–105. Maryknoll, NY: Orbis, 2002.

Gillham, Bill. *Case Study Research Methods*. London: Continuum, 2000.

Goldin, Liliana R., and Brent Metz. "Invisible Converts to Protestantism in Highland Guatemala." In *Crosscurrents in Indigenous Spirituality: Interface of Maya, Catholic and Protestant Worldviews*, edited by Guillermo Cook, 61–81. Leiden: Brill, 1997.

Gosling, David L. "Christian Response within Hinduism." *Religious Studies* 10.4 (1974) 433–39. https://www.jstor.org/stable/20005206.

Griffiths, Bede. *Christian Ashram: Essays towards a Hindu-Christian Dialogue*. London: Darton, Longman & Todd, 1966.

Griffiths, Nicholas, and Fernando Cervantes, eds. *Spiritual Encounters: Intersections between Christianity and Native Religions in Colonial America*. Birmingham: University of Birmingham Press, 1999.

Harvey, Graham, ed. *Indigenous Religions: A Companion*. London: Continuum, 2000.

Heyink, J. W., and TJ. Tymstra. "The Function of Qualitative Research." *Social Indicators Research* 29, no. 3 (1993) 291–305. https://www.jstor.org/stable/27522699.

Hilal, Al-Yahmady Hamed, and Saleh Said Alabri. "Using NVivo for Data Analysis and Qualitative Research." *International Interdisciplinary Journal of Education* 2.2 (2013) 181–86.

Hodgson, Marshall G. S. *The Classical Age of Islam*. The Venture of Islam: Conscience and History in a World Civilization, vol. 1. New ed. Chicago: University of Chicago Press, 1977.

# Bibliography

Hsu, Danny. "Searching for Meaning in a Hybrid and Fractured World: Contemporary Chinese Cultural Identity and Its Implications for Missiology." *Missiology* 45.1 (2017) 103–15. https://doi.org/10.1177/0091829616680647.

Jalal, Ayesha. *Self and Sovereignty: Individual and Community in South Asian Islam since 1850*. Lahore: Sang-e-Meel, 2001.

Kara, Helen. *Research Ethics in the Real World: Euro-Western and Indigenous Perspectives*. Bristol: Policy, 2018.

King, Tomás. "Resilience and Resistance as the Foundations of a Practical Theology for an Oppressed People." PhD diss., Catholic Theological Union, 2008.

Kitiarsa, Pattana. "Beyond Syncretism: Hybridization of Popular Religion in Contemporary Thailand." *Journal of Southeast Asian Studies* 36.3 (2005) 461–87. https://www.jstor.org/stable/20072671.

Kourie, Celia Ellen Teresa. "Crossing Boundaries: The Way of Interspirituality." *Religion & Theology* 18.1–2 (2011) 10–31. https://doi.org/10.1163/157430111X613647.

Kraft, Siv-Ellen. "Sami Indigenous Spirituality: Religion and Nation-Building in Norwegian Sápmi." *Temenos* 45.2 (2009) 179–206. http://search.ebscohost.com/login.aspx?direct=true&db=lsdar&AN=ATLA0001859844&site=ehost-live.

Ku Canche, Facundo, and Team. "Indigenous Theology: A Reformed Protestant Perspective." In *Crosscurrents in Indigenous Spirituality: Interface of Maya, Catholic and Protestant Worldviews*, edited by Guillermo Cook, 189–98. Leiden: Brill, 1997.

Leon-Hartshorn, Iris de. "Renewing Body, Soul, and Mind: Learning from Indigenous Spirituality." *Vision: A Journal for Church and Theology* 17.2 (2016) 24–31. http://press.palni.org/ojs/index.php/vision/article/view/126.

Lopez Hernandez, Eleazar. "Teutlatolli: Speaking about God—Indigenous Theology and Roman Catholicism." In *Crosscurrents in Indigenous Spirituality: Interface of Maya, Catholic and Protestant Worldviews*, edited by Guillermo Cook, 139–70. Leiden: Brill, 1997.

Mananzan, Mary John, and Sun Ai Park. "Emerging Asian Spirituality. Culled from the 'Emerging Spirituality of Asian Women.'" *Women in Action* 3 (1996) 13–18.

Marcos, Sylvia. "Mesoamerican Women's Indigenous Spirituality: Decolonizing Religious Beliefs." *Journal of Feminist Studies in Religion* 25.2 (2009) 25–45. https://doi.org/10.1353/jfs.0.0068.

———, ed. *Women and Indigenous Religions*. Oxford: Praeger, 2010.

McCaffrey, Patrick J. "The Status and Role of the Missionary among the Parkari Kohlis of Pakistan." PhD diss., Catholic Theological Union, 1997.

———. *Towards Inculturation among the Parkari Kholis*. Monograph, Catholic Theological Union, n.d.

McEntee, Rory. "The Religious Quest as Transformative Journey: Interspiritual Religious Belonging and the Problem of Religious Depth." *Open Theology* 3.1 (2017) 613–29.

# Bibliography

McGregor, Bede. "Christ and Hinduism." *The Furrow* 41.1 (1990) 15–18. https://www.jstor.org/stable/27661668.

McKenna, Kathrina, and Rosarie Lordan. *Pakistan Presentation Story Vol. II, 1986–2004*. Rawalpindi, Pakistan: Presentation Sisters, n.d.

Million, Dian. *Therapeutic Nations: Healing in an Age of Indigenous Human Rights*. Tucson: University of Arizona Press, 2013.

Molesky-Poz, Jean. *Contemporary Maya Spirituality: The Ancient Ways Are Not Lost*. Austin: University of Texas Press, 2006.

Mulhall, Brendan. "The Bhagavad Gita and the Kutchi Kohlis." Unpublished essay, April 1989.

———. "Hindu Puja and the Use of Its Symbols in the Eucharist." Unpublished essay, undated.

———. "The Kutchi Kohlis of Sindh and Their Roots." Unpublished essay, undated.

Nayap-Pot, Dalila C. "The Social Role of Maya Women." In *Crosscurrents in Indigenous Spirituality: Interface of Maya, Catholic and Protestant Worldviews*, edited by Guillermo Cook, 101–12. Leiden: Brill, 1997.

O'Brien, John. *The Construction of Pakistani Christian Identity*. Lahore: Research Society of Pakistan, 2006.

———. *The Hope Forever within Us*. Catholic Theology from Pakistan 3. 1st ed. Lahore: Multi Media Affairs, 2018.

———. *The Hope That Is Still with Us*. Catholic Theology from Pakistan 2. 1st ed. Gujranwala, Pakistan: Maktaba-e-Anaveem Pakistan (MAP), 2018.

———. *The Hope That Is within Us*. Catholic Theology from Pakistan 1. 1st ed. Karachi, Pakistan: Catechetical Centre Karachi, 2013.

———. *The Unconquered People: The Liberation of an Oppressed Caste*. Karachi: OUP Pakistan, 2012.

Opas, Minna. "Constituting De-colonializing Horizons: Indigenous Theology, Indigenous Spirituality, and Christianity." *Religious Studies and Theology* 361 (2017) 79–104. https://doi.org/10.1558/rsth.33224.

Ortega, Ofelia. "'A Nation Where Everyone Has a Place': The Chiapas Uprising." In *Crosscurrents in Indigenous Spirituality: Interface of Maya, Catholic and Protestant Worldviews*, edited by Guillermo Cook, 271–92. Leiden: Brill, 1997.

O'Sullivan, Michael. "Authentic Subjectivity and Social Transformation." *HTS Teologiese Studies/Theological Studies* 72.4 (2016) 1–7. http://dx.doi.org/10.4102/hts.v72i4.3452.

———. "'Authenticity and the Identity of Spiritual Studies' Class Notes." Waterford Institute of Technology, 2018.

———. "'Sandra Schneiders on the Academic Study of Spirituality' Class Notes." Waterford Institute of Technology, 2018.

Painadath, Sebastian. "The Integrated Spirituality of the Bhagavad Gita—An Insight for Christians: A Contribution to the Hindu-Christian Dialogue." *Journal of Ecumenical Studies* 39.3–4 (2002) 305–24.

## Bibliography

Ramey, Steven W. "Challenging Definitions: Human Agency, Diverse Religious Practices and the Problems of Boundaries." *Numen* 54.1 (2007) 1–27. https://www.jstor.org/stable/27643243.

Ricoeur, Paul. *Oneself as Another*. Translated by Kathleen Blamey. New ed. Chicago: University of Chicago Press, 1995.

———. *Time and Narrative, Volume 3*. Translated by Kathleen Blamey and David Pellauer. Chicago: University of Chicago Press, 1990.

Rooney, John. *Shadows in the Dark: A History of Christianity in Pakistan up to the 10th Century*. Pakistan Christian History Monograph 1. Rawalpindi: Christian Study Center, 1984.

———. *Symphony on Sands: A History of the Catholic Church in Sind and Baluchistan*. Pakistan Christian History Monograph 6. Rawalpindi: Christian Study Center, 1988.

Schneiders, Sandra. "Approaches to the Study of Christian Spirituality." In *The Blackwell Companion to Christian Spirituality*, edited by Arthur Holder, 15–33. Oxford: Blackwell, 2010.

———. "The Discipline of Christian Spirituality and Catholic Theology." In *Exploring Christian Spirituality: Essays in Honor of Sandra M. Schneiders, IHM*, edited by Bruce H. Lescher and Elizabeth Liebert, 196–212. New York: Paulist, 2006.

———. "A Hermeneutical Approach to the Study of Christian Spirituality." In *Minding the Spirit: The Study of Christian Spirituality*, edited by Elizabeth A. Dreyer and Mark S. Burrows, 49–60. Baltimore: Johns Hopkins University Press, 2005.

———. "Spirituality in the Academy." *Theological Studies* 50 (1989) 676–97.

———. "The Study of Christian Spirituality: Contours and Dynamics of a Discipline." In *Minding the Spirit: The Study of Christian Spirituality*, edited by Elizabeth A. Dreyer and Mark S. Burrows, 5–24. Baltimore: Johns Hopkins University Press, 2005.

Sharma, Arvind. "Hindu Spirituality." *CrossCurrents* 48.1 (1998) 83–88. https://www.jstor.org/stable/24460659.

Sheldrake, Philip. *Spirituality: A Guide for the Perplexed*. London: Bloomsbury Academic, 2014.

Shimoni, Baruch. "Cultural Borders, Hybridization, and a Sense of Boundaries in Thailand, Mexico, and Israel." *Journal of Anthropological Research* 62.2 (2006) 217–34.

Shimoni, Baruch, and Harriet Bergmann. "Managing in a Changing World: From Multiculturalism to Hybridization: The Production of Hybrid Management Cultures in Israel, Thailand, and Mexico." *Academy of Management Perspectives* 20.3 (2006) 76–89.

Smith, Dennis A. "Crosscurrents in Indigenous Spirituality: Interface of Maya, Catholic and Protestant Worldviews." *International Review of Mission* 87.347 (1998) 575–77. http://search.ebscohost.com/login.aspx?direct=true&db=lsdar&AN=ATLA0000357863&site=ehost-live.

## Bibliography

Smith, Linda Tuhiwai. *Decolonizing Methodologies: Research and Indigenous Peoples*. London: Zed, 2008.

Stock, Frederick, and Margaret Stock. *People Movements in the Punjab: With Special Reference to the United Presbyterian Church*. South Pasadena, CA: William Carey Library, 1975.

Taylor, Steven J., et al. *Introduction to Qualitative Research Methods: A Guidebook and Resource*. 4th ed. New Jersey: John Wiley & Sons, 2016.

Teasdale, Wayne. *The Mystic Heart: Discovering a Universal Spirituality in the World's Religions*. Novato, CA: New World Library, 2001.

Victor, Mohan. "General Survey of the Katchi Kohli Illaqa." Unpublished report written for the parish in Tando Allahyar, 2001.

Vilaça, Aparecida, and Robin M. Wright, eds. *Native Christians: Modes and Effects of Christianity among Indigenous Peoples of the Americas*. Surrey: Ashgate, 2009.

Vrajaprana, Pravrajika. "Contemporary Spirituality and the Thinning of the Sacred: A Hindu Perspective." *CrossCurrents* 50.1/2 (2000) 248–56. https://www.jstor.org/stable/24461258.

Wertz, Frederick J., et al. *Five Ways of Doing Qualitative Analysis: Phenomenological Psychology, Grounded Theory, Discourse Analysis, Narrative Research, and Intuitive Inquiry*. New York: Guilford, 2011.

Young, William G. *Days of Small Things?* Pakistan Christian History Monograph 8. Rawalpindi, Pakistan: Christian Study Center, 1991.

www.ingramcontent.com/pod-product-compliance
Lightning Source LLC
Chambersburg PA
CBHW070511090426
42735CB00012B/2731